With all my love to my husband, Jeff Haas, who coined the term Free Range Priest, and supports my ministry in every way.

Introduction

I walk into St. Anna's[1] and breathe the familiar scent of incense and wax that is worn into the wood carvings and cool gray stone. The light is dim, filtered in jewel tones through the stained glass windows, centuries old. I love this tidy, stately space, and as I drop my prayer book in the seat reserved for the worship leader, I step up into the understated pulpit and survey the empty pews. The church is beautiful - perfect architecture to capture the traditional Sunday worship that will start in an hour or so. Those who will gather here are sustained and comforted by this expression of the Christian faith of the Episcopal Church. As the priest, I am clothed right now in a black suit and white clergy collar, but soon I will put on my robe and stole for our liturgical celebration, and we will all take our places and know our parts. The world will disappear for a little while, and we will let ourselves enter God's time and Kingdom, reminding ourselves where, and to whom, we really belong.

The world won't really disappear, of course, and if I am being honest, it will hardly even notice we are here. When the service starts, there will only be a couple dozen more people out there before me when I preach than there are now in the empty sanctuary. There will be hundreds more outside, strolling the sidewalks of this bustling town, driving down the busy street where the church is located, cycling to the coffee shop next door, walking their dogs to the park across the street. Sunday morning is busy here, but not inside the sturdy walls of this place.

And I am not the priest who belongs to this congregation. They do not pay me a salary, because frankly, they can't afford to. I am here as so-called "Sunday supply", preaching and celebrating the Eucharist for a fixed fee, and then I will be gone, somewhere else next Sunday. This congregation will take care of most of their modest needs themselves, calling on clergy when they must and paying them as they can. And I will live my priestly vocation wherever it calls me, from church to church and, increasingly, outside these heavy wooden doors and into the streets beyond them, literally and virtually.

And the world rolls by, sometimes forgetting the church is here, overlooking its riches right in front of the parks and coffee shops, and losing the connection between ancient beliefs and modern life. Many have forgotten, or have never even been aware, of the grounding that religious belief can give our lives, the sense that it can help make of matters big and small - relationships and work, life and death, peace and love. Many people, if not most, no longer go to church every Sunday, or belong to a congregation, or practice the Christian faith. Or any faith at all. Perhaps this makes no difference to their lives, but it makes a difference to me - I have good news to share about the transforming love of God, and I feel a longing to make it known to all who have not heard it.

Being a priest is, to me, the most important job in the world. Serving a congregation on Sunday, and every other day besides, is what I always believed I was called to do by God, what I studied for, and what I have devoted my life to. This call was upheld by the Holy Spirit and the people of the Episcopal Church when they ordained me. And 20 years ago when I began this journey, I never even considered that I would be anything but a parish priest, employed by one congregation or another for my whole career.

It never would have occurred to me then that at the height of my experience and energy for sharing the stories, traditions and sacraments of the Christian faith, I would not be doing so as a rector - a full-time, salaried, ordained minister in a congregation. I could not have known how soon and how quickly the church would be pushed from the center of daily life for so many individuals and communities, and the impact this would have on my beloved vocation and institution. And I know - from being in and around the church for so long, that few congregations anticipated this. Even today, I think that many people in the pews and many clergy who serve them are not fully aware of the extent that the changes in the church and around it have led us here: to the place where we really cannot sustain the model of full-time clergy in every congregation, much less strong mission beyond the church doors. I think we still live our daily lives and ministries as if that time is far off, or may never happen.

But that day has come. There are approximately 6,553 congregations in the Episcopal Church. According to extensive research done by the church in 2014, just over half of them (54.4%) employ at least one full-time priest. Another 34.5% are served by clergy half-time or less. That means about 11% of congregations - 721 of them across the church - have no salaried clergy at all[2]. Most of the congregations with no paid clergy are small, and almost all of the congregations with more than one full-time priest are large, which is no real surprise. It is not hard to conclude that smaller congregations would have more clergy serving them if they could afford to pay for their ministry.

Not surprisingly, it also works the other way around. There are just over 5,000 priests working full-time in the Episcopal Church, out of 7,271 active (paid) priests overall. At the turn of the 21st century, there were just over 6,000[3], so we lost 1,000 full-time positions in 15 years. This means that roughly 2,100 priests - about one third of all who are active - are serving half-time or less[4]. We have no way of knowing for certain if this is because they choose this, or because full-time ministry positions are unavailable. But it is not hard to extrapolate, based on the data, that more clergy would work full-time if those positions were available.

The Episcopal Church - the smallest mainline Christian denomination - is hardly alone in dealing with these tensions. Even the largest denomination in the country, by far - the Southern Baptist Convention - reported losing 1.5 million members, from 17 to 15.5 million, between 2013 and 2014.[5] The United Methodist Church, in their own research, also discovered fewer full-time positions for clergy and a leap in the number of Methodist clergy working part-time or doing only Sunday supply[6]. My aim here is to paint a picture rather than offer endless statistics, but even the most cursory glance at denominational research shows steep decline across the board.

Secular research makes the same case from the opposite perspective. Gallup does excellent polling and analysis about many subjects, and has looked into Americans' religious habits extensively. According to Gallup.com, those in the U.S. who identify as Christian dropped by 29% between 1948 and 2015, and churchgoing dropped 16% between 1992 and 2015 alone. Even among those Americans who do still attend church or synagogue (54% of the population in 2015), only 36% of them reported attending worship in the previous seven days[7]. There is simply no way around the fact that the number of Christians practicing their religion in America continues to fall, congregations continue to lose members, and clergy struggle to find full-time congregational employment. For those of us who are clergy or committed lay people, this is troubling news, and while much is made of this, it is hard to figure a way to change these trends. And so for the most part we continue on with business as usual, doing the things that have made the traditional church a center of spiritual growth and good news for all. But the tension still lingers.

It seems that here in the early 21st century we find ourselves in an uneasy triangle: people in congregations are finding it increasingly difficult to sustain the life and the rhythm of the traditional denominational church; the population in general, still celebrating and struggling with the stuff of life but increasingly unconvinced that God has anything to do with this, live mostly outside of a faith community; and those of us who were ordained to care for those both inside and outside of the church walls find fewer ways to sustain ourselves as we try to live this call. We each have things the others need - resources, energy, faith - but we are failing to connect in the ways we have in the past. An uncertain and increasing tension remains - the church can't change enough to appeal to those outside of it who need it; the world can't see the gifts of faith; and the clergy cannot both save the traditional church and evangelize the masses. It seems like something needs to give, for the sake of us all.

We are trying to change, of course. Congregations across the country and across Christian denominations are meeting in new places, including online. They are reaching new populations, including those who most need support. They are speaking out against injustice and advocating for those in need. Clergy and lay leaders are deeply involved in much of this ministry, which is faithful, important, and often life-changing. And yet it does not change either church statistics or church survival rates. This is because the basic model of traditional churches is still the same, relying on a place to gather, a clergy person to lead, and a congregation to worship and organize ministry, and pay for it all. This basic model hasn't really changed, and isn't likely to. But it no longer suffices on its own - for the faithful, the faith-seekers, or the clergy.

For the first half of my career as a priest, I hardly considered any of this at all. I served as one of three full-time priests at a large parish in a very large urban area, and then I served as one of two full-time priests at a very active mid-sized congregation in a small city. Once I became a rector, or senior priest, of my own congregation, I began to be enlightened about the struggles of congregations as they faced a future of emptier pews, tighter budgets, and suspicions of irrelevance.

When I served on a bishop's staff, essentially as an 'in-house' church consultant, I began to understand that the congregational/evangelical/clergy leadership tension triangle was not just being experienced in a few places, but in many places. Maybe even most. Not just in small congregations, but often mid-sized and even larger parishes, where even though more people are present, involved and committed to the life of the church, there are not as many as there have been in decades past. Congregations cannot figure out how to change to appeal to their own children and grandchildren, the vast majority of whom are no longer interested in being there. They worry more and more about supporting their clergy. And clergy worry about their jobs, both in the vocational and the financial sense. 'How will I do the work God has called me to do? And how will I support myself and my family while I do it?' These questions haunt many I have spent time with.

I was haunted as well, by the desire to live fully into my very traditional priestly vocation, and the pull to be part of re-imagining what church could be and do and grow into in the future. Finding myself more and more experienced with the congregational/clergy tensions, I felt less desire to be part of them, but more curious about how they might be addressed. I wanted to talk about changing the church institution, but not the entire structure. I wanted to do more than talk, actually - I wanted to experience this change. And more than experience it, I wanted to expand it to include experiencing what it is like to reach those who would never dream of coming to church.

So I became a Free Range Priest.

Yes, like the chicken. My husband made up the name, because he saw how I was suddenly free of the boundaries of one particular stone structure and able to interact with many congregations. He also saw how I could work on the denominational level, and how I could move between and beyond denominations. And he saw how I could interact with those outside of church, in person and online, and how in all of these interactions, I was still very much a priest, I had simply become one whose ministry happens in many different locations.

Let me take a moment to say that if you are not familiar with church language, or you are part of a denomination in which ordination is not a sacrament, then the word "priest" may not describe what you are or the clergy people you know. In terms of this book, that's ok. I am a Free Range *Priest*, but even if you are more of a Free Range Pastor or a Free Range Deacon, the concept is pretty much the same: How does an ordained person re-think ministry in a time and place when fewer congregations can pay for a professional clergy salary and more people need God and don't look for help from the church? In other words, how can we live into our ministry where and how we are called, and also support ourselves while doing so? These questions transcend denominations, maybe even faith categories. And that's what this book - and my ministry - are about.

Free Range Priest is not trying to change the basic model of church (building/congregation/clergy), so much as re-imagine how the clergy part might work. Instead of asking congregations to change who they are, or clergy to change what we do, what if all that changes is how and where clergy serve the church, and how we get paid to do it?

Frankly, this is already happening, and I will document some of the Free Range Priests I know in these pages. But I think we still imagine "supply priests" as the retired or the exception, and ordained writers more as bloggers than clergy, and hospice chaplains who also teach as "bi-vocational" rather than "Free Range Priests". Why does this matter? Because I think that as we focus on how clergy serve the church inside and outside of the congregation, in a variety of roles, we can see how the one congregation/one salaried clergy model is being transcended, and that this is good for congregations and clergy, and for sharing the Gospel beyond church walls.

Thinking like a Free Range Priest means that we can give congregations the ordained ministry they need, but not more than they can afford. This means more freedom and growth for congregations, and hopefully less stress. It also means that clergy can find ways to live out our vocation in a variety of settings simultaneously, which means we may feel more free to be who we are called to be. It means we are free to meet the unchurched world in new and exciting ways. And it means we can get paid to do ministry, even if all of our salary does not come from one congregation. I like to say that I am kind of like an Uber driver for your spiritual experience!

If you are like me, you see congregations struggle and want to help them survive and thrive. You see the wider world forgetting the Christian faith and you want to help it know how love and forgiveness, peace and reconciliation can be found and lived through following Jesus. You look at your own call to ordained ministry, and want to help answer it in a way that deepens the roots of God's Kingdom, inside the church walls and beyond. This is exactly how I became a Free Range Priest, and why I think the concept, small as it is, contributes to the growth of the church and the growth of ministry, lay and ordained.

Every time I walk into a place like St. Anna's, I am filled with the sense that I belong right here, part of the tradition of worship and prayer that goes back centuries, and I want to be part of preserving this way of life. Every time I go online and write about God in my marriage, or forgiveness at the grocery store, I feel the same sense of purpose. When I travel to talk with groups about how the rapidly changing new century is the very best time to be a Christian - even when it feels like nothing is the same - I feel the same holiness under my feet as when I stand on the steps of the wooden pulpit in the small but solid stone church. Connecting all of these experiences and gathering them into one ministry is how I am becoming a Free Range Priest.

This book is the story of what Free Range Priest ministry can look like, why it is important, how it can help congregations big and small to thrive, and how it can re-vitalize evangelism. The story is aimed at clergy, because the Free Range Priest vision is about ordained ministry in the church and the world.

I also hope this story is interesting to lay members of Christian congregations, whether you are experiencing some of the tension I have described or not. Those in denominational leadership or any other kind of church administration may find it interesting in their work of supporting ministry in a wider context.

I really hope this story is compelling to those who are not Christian, or not members of a congregation, but who do have questions about God in your life and wonder if there are places besides church to ask them (there are!). It is the beginning of a story that I hope has many future chapters about how the church in the world is growing and changing, and how we are called to be a part of this.

1. The Work of Clergy

What is it that a priest actually does?

As I said, being a priest is the most important job in the world, as far as I am concerned. But surprisingly, it can be hard to describe what we actually *do*. Being Free Range does not effect the *Priest* part of my vocation, so as we begin the journey of re-imagining where and how clergy work, I thought it might be good to touch on what that work is. Again, if *priest* does not apply in your context, then *minister, pastor*, etc.

When I worked with small congregations looking for new clergy, I would usually meet with a representative group and draw up some hopes and expectations - what kind of salary they could offer, what kind of pastor they were looking for, things like this. I would start with this question: "What exactly does a priest do?"

And always - I mean I have done this at least 20 times and there were no exceptions - always, I was met with blank stares. Complete silence. They had never considered this in detail before. Inevitably, there was some uncomfortable silence, everyone looking at someone else to speak. And then one person would tentatively raise their hand and say, "Everything?"

Exactly. This is the answer, most of the time. I am amazed at how ingrained it is in the heads of clergy and congregations alike that a priest basically comes with the church territory, does everything that is necessary to do, and maybe a few things that are not strictly necessary. Of course a priest, or any other ordained person, serves primarily to lead worship, preach, and administer the sacraments on Sunday. After that, priests take care of the congregation pastorally - helping them understand God's love in their lives during good times and bad. Clergy teach and pray and visit and help with outreach and administration. They oversee the music, the bulletin, the seasonal schedule and the training of others who serve in the church. That adds up to a lot of things that clergy do.

But those of us who are church people, lay and ordained, know it rarely ends there. The priest is usually the one who answers the phone or opens the door or sweeps up after everyone has left or sets up appointments with the people who fix the plumbing and the roof, especially in congregations too small to pay anyone else to do those things. Which, these days, is most congregations.

Priests, it turns out, do usually do *everything*.

One year, I even spent a summer being a cat rescue specialist.

The church I worked for in Kansas was an urban parish adjacent to a vacant lot. Beyond that was an apartment complex where people with very limited incomes lived. An older woman, who probably had ten cats in her tiny one-bedroom, also faithfully left food out every day for the feral cats in the neighborhood. Of course, it did not take long for those cats to become a herd (or a flock, or whatever you call a large colony of cats), and of course they started breeding like… feral cats.

So one spring, we had an explosion of kitten births. Because our church had a lovely enclosed courtyard, the momma cats found this to be an excellent nursery. Each day we would arrive to see a new little batch of tiny furry things. It was out of control, yet we couldn't bear to see harm come to them. Some of the kittens became abandoned after their moms did not return from their nightly food run, and so we 'temporarily' brought them into the parish office, where the administrator and I bottle fed them kitten formula. We kept them in cardboard copier paper boxes and tried to get people to adopt them. We did send our bookkeeper home with one, after she confirmed that this was not an ethical violation for receiving an inappropriate gift! I brought a whole box full of kittens into church at announcement time during the service and offered them up to good homes (it was hilarious - in unison, every man turned to every woman and child in the congregation and said, "No.")

Eventually, we got the kittens adopted (and kept one "church cat"). Then we were faced with the reality that this might happen again. So my parish administrator and I spent an autumn week with a cat rescue group, staying up late at night, trapping the adult cats, spay/neutering and vaccinating them, and releasing them. Eventually, our feral cat neighbors were reduced to a manageable number and stopped giving birth on our grounds.

I digress into this long tale to clarify how easy it is for a clergyperson in a congregation to get caught up in a whole lot of work that has nothing at all to do with why we were ordained in the first place. In this congregation, I was the sole priest, one of a handful of actual employees, and the only one on the grounds pretty much every day (I once also kept the boiler from exploding on New Year's Day because I had just happened to stop by to make sure the doors were locked and found the heat off. Then I had to call emergency boiler guys on New Year's Day. But that is a whole different story...)

The summer and fall I spent doing cat rescue is just one example of things I spent countless hours doing that were definitely not in the priest job description, while doing all the other things priests get paid to do. I also did them because no one else was going to do them (except my saintly parish administrator, who was another person working way more than she should). If I didn't get certain things done, I felt, they weren't going to get done. And then there were going to be some really big problems, like feral cats overrunning our property.

Since I was the only one around most of the time, it seemed fitting that I would be the person to take on the strange and the mundane tasks that came with the territory of a church building and property. My cat story is unique (as far as I know...) but the nature of it is not. With the way we set up the relationship between clergy and congregation, it is natural to assume that clergy do *everything* that needs to be done around the church, regardless of whether it is work for which they get paid - or the kind or work we are actually needed for.

Back in the rooms where I would sit and talk with small congregations, this is the reason for their silence at first. Yet once they had thought about it a bit, and talked about it, it never took them long to come up with a list of what the priest really does. This is especially true when I was talking with them about part-time work, ten or 20 hours a week.

"If you only had this limited amount of a priest's time, what would you want them to do with it?" I would ask. I would push them, and we would all assume that no clergy work more hours than they are paid for (a big assumption).

Again, when faced with this question, congregations were uniformly clear in their answers: Sunday worship, visiting the sick, being there when they needed spiritual counsel, and burying members of the congregation when they died. Once introduced to the theoretical idea that they might only get to see their priest a handful of hours a week, these three things were very much at the top of their list, every time.

This is not really so surprising. Our congregations want us to do the very things that we want to do as clergy: pray, lead worship, bring God's presence into people's lives at times of uncertainty, transition, suffering, and death. They want us to bear the sacraments and tradition of the Christian faith into their lives and into the world.

I am pretty sure that's what most of us who are ordained want to spend our time doing as well.

Even though there are lots of tasks in the big category called *everything*, clergy are actually called to do a very important, very specific set of tasks. As we start talking about what it means to be a Free Range Priest, it seems important to simply start with what it means to be a priest (or minister, pastor, etc.). Clarifying our role as clergy helps clarify what we need to focus our time and energy on, and also why this is so important. What clergy do is often hard to describe, because much of it is spiritual in nature. But that is exactly why it matters so much - our work ties heaven and earth, the mystic and the mundane, all together, every day. So I thought it would be helpful as we start to set out a little bit of how we do what we do, and why we can't forget its value.

Set apart to serve the church and the world

All of us who are ordained, no matter how locally we serve, or in what denomination (if any), are first and foremost ordained in the Christian faith. From Biblical times, certain leaders were set apart especially for specific tasks related to worshiping God, overseeing the life of the Christian community, and caring for the poor and vulnerable. We have different titles for clergy (*priest, pastor, minister, bishop, deacon, preacher,* etc.), but every expression of the Christian faith has some way of designating specific religious roles and preparing and commissioning certain people for them.

In the Episcopal Church, priests, deacons, and bishops each take different ordination vows. In the case of priests, we are asked by the church to promise, in part, that we will:

"Proclaim the Gospel by word and deed (and fashion your life with its precepts); love and serve the people among you; preach, administer the sacraments, pronounce God's blessing and forgiveness of sins."

This is a pretty good outline of the kinds of things that we are called to do in our daily

lives as clergy, as it is both fairly specific and broadly interpreted. The last parts - preaching, sacraments, blessing and pronouncing forgiveness - are generally (though not always) done on Sunday morning in the context of worship. The first three - proclaiming the Gospel, patterning our lives around it, and loving and serving the people among us - are things we do every day, in a variety of different ways.

This is another way that priests end up doing too much. "Proclaiming the Gospel" can look like teaching people to read and interpret Scripture, and it can also look like protesting unjust laws or handing out food and water after a disaster. Loving and serving others can mean counseling them, taking them for coffee, playing basketball with them, even helping to control the feral cat population in their neighborhood. So when we stop and ask ourselves, "Is this really what a priest is ordained to do?," there are very many ways to answer "yes" to this question.

So it may be easier to ask the question in reverse - "Is it necessary to be ordained to do this particular work?" Here, I think, we are able to answer "Yes" more clearly about some things (administering sacraments, for example), and for others we can at least say "It is pretty important." Things like preaching, for example, fall into this category. It is not strictly necessary for a person to be ordained in order to preach; there are many fine lay preachers. But it is not advisable for someone to give a sermon without preparation - to have a strong background in Biblical study, a deep prayer life, a clear understanding of what it means to declare good news - and clergy very often come with these qualifications. So it is a good idea to be ordained in order to preach, even if it is not unique to the clergy vocation.

You may wonder why it is so important to clarify what a priest (or other clergy person) does. It is sort of like clarifying what a firefighter does. We all know the general answer - they fight fires - but do we often ask ourselves what they do all day? Not really, because when something is on fire, we really need them. The rest of the time we assume they are generally working on fire prevention and safety, and preparation/clean up after fires. And making chili (I kid). Not everything they do is highly skilled, but the one skill they have is the one we really need.

The same is true for clergy, and there is a danger that the world might be forgetting this. Clergy are ordained to be the living vessels and symbols of God's love and God's presence in our world, and to do whatever work we need to in order to make God's love and Jesus' proclamation of Good News known to everyone. Most people don't think about our work, unless there is a "fire", a spiritual question or crisis or need that leads them to seek God, and someone who has the background and qualifications to help them find God, and walk more closely with Jesus.

At that moment, they need a priest and nothing but a priest.

In our increasingly unchurched world, however, there is a false sense of security that there will be no spiritual "fires" - or if there are, then we can put them out ourselves. People think they have all the spiritual answers they need, or they can connect themselves to God's love, or they can just connect to love and not worry about the God part.

As clergy, we need to know this is not true. The absolute value of what we do is that we believe for people, and we insist that God is real, God's Kingdom is at hand, and that this is the best news in the world. Many, many people do not want to hear this, or have no interest in believing it. It is our job to believe for them anyway, and to know in our bones that this is of enormous value.

There is no one else in the world forgiving sins in the name of the Lord, pronouncing God's blessing on individuals and communities, and consecrating bread and wine as the sacrament of Holy Eucharist (or Communion) besides us. If we don't do this, it doesn't get done. There may be many people who don't care if this work gets done, or don't see its worth, but this does not mean it is not worthy. Quite the opposite.

There may be no other time in history, since the very beginning of the Church itself, that what we do is so important. When so many people are disconnected from the life of the church, it becomes more important for us to make that connection. We cannot let the world forget the power of God's love and God's Kingdom, manifest among us in this time and place.

And we have to balance the importance of our work with the tendency to make it *everything*, which could then just make it *anything*. There is the danger, especially for clergy, that we will so diffuse the idea of loving God and our neighbor with just generally being good people that we lose the connection to Christianity itself. We need to be able to be theological interpreters. We need to be able to translate the work we do through the lens of the Gospel. And we need to be brave enough to step back from work that cannot be translated in this way, and to support others doing it.

Using myself as an example again, I will say that trapping feral cats, even bottle-feeding them, falls squarely into the category of not being priestly ministry. That might have been good work, it might have accomplished something that improved the lives of the community (and the cats), but I cannot tie it directly to sharing the Gospel, and surely no one involved with that particular adventure came any closer to following Jesus because of it.

If I were working in a congregation again, I would not engage in these tasks. I might encourage others to do so; I might even encourage them to find meaning as Christian disciples in it (being stewards of God's kingdom, for example), but I could not really see the actual work as being the ministry I was ordained to do. Maybe others could, but I would ask them to explain how - and show their work!

Clergy share the Good News and equip disciples

Not all religions are inherently evangelical, but for Christians, this is the basic feature of our faith. To want to share the good news of the Gospel, to want to encourage and sustain others as they grow in their faith, this is what we are all about. The very last thing Jesus said to us when he walked the earth is "go and make disciples of all the world" (Matthew 28:19). That is the basic job description of all Christians.

And while Jesus didn't single out ordained people for this job - he seemed to be speaking to us all - when we think about what it means to be clergy in today's world, evangelism and disciple-making is at the top of the list of things that really are our business. Lay people are often tentative at best about sharing their faith. We have had decades of cultural indoctrination, which taught us that it is bad form to impose, or even discuss our religious tendencies outside of church. Sometimes even inside of church we can be a bit shy about talking about what we really believe.

Even though we should all be making disciples, clergy have the background, the training, and hopefully the comfort level to do so. This manifests itself in a variety of ways, from encouraging the prayer lives and curiosity of those in the pews to talking about our own faith journeys online to sharing social media about what it means to be Christian. How we are engaged in evangelism can vary widely, but the fact that we are engaged is a very important part of our job as clergy, and one we should be doing with great regularity.

It is also our business to help encourage lay people in their own evangelical efforts. We can coach them in their own faith, and their own comfort with sharing their journey with those they meet along the way. We can show them that talking about religion, especially sharing our own beliefs and stories about God, is perfectly appropriate, and inviting others to church can be a very welcome gesture. Even talking with close friends and family can be daunting for lay people sometimes - parishioners often lament to me how their children and grandchildren no longer go to church, for instance, and how they don't know how to broach the subject with them. As clergy, we have the zeal and the skill to be evangelists, and to help others live into their evangelism as well.

Most of us who are ordained have a story to tell about what led us to this particular vocation. Many of these stories involve being called by God and/or experiencing the love of Jesus. Or they might involve how we met someone else, often quite randomly, who shared their faith with us in such a way that we were inspired on our own Christian journey. This makes us very much like those first disciples, eager to share what we have come to know and reaching out to others to make sure they know, too. These stories, combined with our background, training and experience, are very valuable parts of our unique gifts as ordained clergy, and invaluable in helping others on their own paths of discipleship when we have the courage to share them.

Clergy live and teach the Christian faith

What do Christians believe?

This is another question that can lead to awkward silence in a room, especially in a room of Christians. Or clergy. This question seems so simple, but it is really hard to answer. With fewer and fewer Americans raised in or practicing the faith, the basic tenets of our Scripture, creeds, sacraments and traditions can be easy to forget. Even those who are in our pews may get a little fuzzy about why Jesus died on the cross, or how we define sin. Sometimes we settle into a place where we understand that God loves us and we should love each other, and we don't get into the details too much.

Christian Smith, a religion sociologist, coined a term to explain this kind of thinking - Moralistic Therapeutic Deism (MTD[8]). Smith did in-depth research about the theology of teenagers, and discovered a belief system widely held across faith traditions and beyond. Basically, they believe God is good, God wants us to be good, and God sends good people to heaven when they die.

Many adults believe this, too, whether they claim to be Christians, Muslims, Jews, or no religion at all. What is troubling about this is it skips the specific beliefs of the Christian faith (and other faiths). Smith says, "the language - and therefore experience - of Trinity, holiness, sin, grace, justification, sanctification, church, Eucharist, and heaven and hell appear, among most Christian teenagers in the United States at the very least, to be being supplanted by the language of happiness, niceness, and earned heavenly reward[9]."

For those of us who are ordained in a very specific faith, follow Jesus exclusively and believe that doing so is about the salvation of the world and everyone in it, this is difficult news. For us, it is not that we are saying "follow Jesus or go to hell," as we sometimes experience in more fundamentalist corners. It is, instead, "follow Jesus and know heaven on earth - God's Kingdom - right now." Because we believe in sin, forgiveness, and redemption through Jesus, and because we believe in the life, death and resurrection of Jesus as fully God and fully human, we have a lot of very specific good news to share. But we really have to share it specifically.

It is also hard to counter-balance the Moralistic Therapeutic Deism belief system if we don't have a base camp of Christianity that reaches large groups of people regularly. With fewer and fewer people in church on Sunday, we are necessarily reaching fewer and fewer people with our faith. And even then, we may not be reaching them with actual religious instruction.

Clergy want to share what we know, because what we know is the Scripture, history, tradition and theology of following Jesus that has changed the world (and is still changing it) and transformed billions of lives. It is a specific set of beliefs that is centered on sin and forgiveness, reconciliation and redemption, self-giving love, death and resurrection. Clergy are equipped, and required, to teach the faith and correct theological error, which is badly needed in the world, and the church, today.

Clergy foster community and care for those in need

Community is a word that is overused - and badly used. We don't live in a neighborhood, we live in a "residential community"; the running group I belong to is an "athletic community"; I am part of several "online communities" and other "communities" related to where I habitually eat or shop. I am not trying to disparage as I point this out - there is no doubt that in a world that feels more and more isolating, we have an increased craving to be together, to bond over a shared interest or activity, to feel like we are not alone. As of the 2012 US Census, almost 32 million people live alone in this country, 27% of the population, which is a 10 percent increase since 1970[10]. The marriage rate is decreasing and the marrying age is increasing[11]. We are, as a population, redefining the traditional ideas of what community and family mean, and in a lot of ways we are becoming more of a collection of individuals than a number of groups.

Church has always been a place of community. The very first disciples shared food, hospitality, and money as they formed the new Christian faith (see the Acts of the Apostles for more on this). Christianity is about being brothers and sisters in Christ, and even Jesus said, "whoever does the will of my Father in heaven is my brother and sister and mother" (Matthew 12:49). One of the great tenets of following Jesus is that you cannot do it alone. Jesus himself called disciples who were (mostly) unrelated to each other and from very different walks of life. The greatest commandment he gave us is "love God with all your heart and soul and mind, and love your neighbor as yourself'" (Matthew 22:37-39). With this as our work, it is guaranteed we are never alone! Not mention that Jesus was always noticing the poor, and those in need, and wondering aloud whose job it is to care for them (hint: all of us). We are never to forget that we are brothers and sisters in this way, too: called to bear each others' burdens.

Clergy, then, are very interested in creating and sustaining community in the name of Jesus. Eating, praying, worshiping and sharing sacraments together are the basic ways we do this, but of course there are many ways this can be carried out. Again, this is not a unique calling - all Christians, whether ordained or not, are meant to be in community - but for clergy this is the basic canvas and framework of everything else we do.

One thing I have noticed in congregations is how they function as a social outlet for people who do not have so many of them. I have known many parishioners who were single, didn't have children or a wide circle of friends, and for whom the community of the church was the only major social outlet they had. It was where they spent holidays and commemorated milestones and had meaningful conversations. If not for the ministry of the church, these people would be much more alone.

Congregations are also usually multi-generational spaces, and this adds dimension to the kind of community church can be. Lots of other communities that are formed around an activity or shared interest, such as an athletic team or a book club, have much less diversity around age, gender or background. When I was a young single adult, the only time I ever really interacted with children and people of retirement age was at church. This was extremely meaningful to me in terms of enriching my sense of community, helping me better understand the experience and viewpoints of others.

Creating community is also a place for discernment in terms of our call as ordained people. Not every part of it is exclusively the role of clergy, and some of it is better done by lay people. Celebrating the Eucharist is definitely the center of what we are called to do. Hosting a party may or may not be part of our job description - it depends on what the party is for, where it happens and why, etc. Christian community can look like bringing people of differing backgrounds together, it can be organizing an event that others take part in, it can be a learning opportunity. But somewhere in it should be the specific message that this community is in the name of Jesus, and formed intentionally as a Christian act. This is what grounds us and this is why bringing people together is so important to us.

'Community' can mean many things, and as Christians we are called beyond just gathering together for the comfort of not being alone. Our unity is always in the service of our faith. The church provides opportunity for people to gather in the name of love and forgiveness, gentleness and hospitality, to care for each and every person as a child of God. Clergy are called to help us all see each other as neighbors, to help communities model nonviolence, sharing resources, respecting the dignity of all. We have a unique perspective as Christian faith leaders to help foster and maintain this kind of community.

Clergy stand for justice and question the status quo

Archbishop Desmond Tutu is a an activist who stood against Apartheid discrimination in South Africa, and continues to be involved in many social movements that promote peace and justice today[12]. And he is an ordained clergyperson. Martin Luther King, Jr. was first and foremost a Baptist minister and stellar preacher, and his faith led him to give his life for civil rights in the 1960s[13]. The Presiding Bishop of the Episcopal Church, whose father marched with Dr. King, has himself spoken powerfully and eloquently against injustice and for the rights of the poor, the oppressed, and the voiceless. The Rt. Rev. Michael B. Curry is an extraordinary clergyperson whose calling has made him a public figure of peace and reconciliation in the church and the world[14]. Not all of us are so well-known, but those who follow Jesus are those who know very well that Jesus said "blessed are the poor" and "blessed are you when you are persecuted for righteousness" sake.' (Matthew 5-7). Part of our job description as clergy is to speak and act against injustice or any social wrong, and to protect the vulnerable and advocate for the poor.

Christianity has always been counter-cultural. Early Christians held their goods and property in common, they refused military service and were not allowed to sue one another. The church, at its best, has been a refuge and a haven from the extremes of worldly wealth and power, and it has been an advocate for those in dire situations - poverty, enslavement, victimized by natural and manmade calamities, those in prison or oppressed. Being a Christian means standing for values that include putting others' needs before our own and loving and forgiving those who do us wrong. We are to witness to our faith by our actions as well as by our words.

Clergy are especially called to this witness, as examples and encouragers. Often, especially in today's cultural climate, there is fear and concern about being too political and what that means for clergy expressing their opinions about injustice and intolerance in public life. Of course, there is a difference between *politics* and *political* and it is this: Christians in general, and clergy in particular need to take special care not to equate our particular view on any social matter with Christianity itself. Thus to say, "Jesus is a liberal" (or conservative) is to hijack our religion for the sake of a secular viewpoint, and it is aligning the very will of God with our own opinions, thereby casting anyone who disagrees with us as someone who disagrees with God (not to mention putting ourselves in the position of knowing God's opinion!). This not only alienates our neighbors who disagree with us, it works against the tenets of our faith which insist that no one is outside of the love of God.

On the other hand, to be political is to take notice of our neighbors and the conditions that they live in, and to be ready to help change those conditions if they are intolerable. Jesus did do this when he pointed out the poor widow giving away her last penny (Luke 21:1-4), when he ate with tax collectors and sinners, and when he said, "whatever you do to the least of these, you do to me" (Matthew 25:40), among many other of his words and actions. To speak against injustice and hatred, to speak for those who have no voice, to suggest that the Kingdom of God is a place where there is no fear or suffering and we are called to recognize that even here and now, this is the work of faithful Christian. Without endorsing any particular way of solving these issues as solely "God's way'", but exhorting all those who follow Jesus that we must work for peace, love and forgiveness, we are upholding our religious values without confusing them with our political opinion.

This is one way in which clergy are particularly called to this work: it is very easy to start confusing our politics with our religion. Our training and formation as clergy put us in the position of understanding the difference, and helping others to do so as well. Lay people are just as called as clergy to help change the world in generous and loving ways aligned with our faith. Clergy can support them by helping to translate the religious principles that undergird our activism. Without hope in God's Kingdom, we would not have the energy or the motivation to stand against the forces of evil, or the ability to remember we are all brothers and sisters, even when we are at odds with one another or lost in confusion and darkness. Only God can help us find our way in political and social disagreements and crises. Clergy are especially called to help us all remember this and discern our actions as followers of Jesus.

Clergy spend time in church

Even though there are not as many of us actually in church as there used to be, for clergy, this is our happy place. I have never met an ordained person who didn't love church - music, prayer, worship, gathering, the building and architecture, the special occasions and holy days. We all have our own way of doing it, and we absolutely have our preferences for how it should be done, but mostly there is no place we would rather be.

Clergy are, in fact, primarily ordained to lead worship - to pray and preach publicly, to preside at sacraments, to baptize, marry, and conduct funerals. When you think of a clergyperson, it is hard not to think of someone in robes, standing in the front of a congregation. Of course other ministers participate in and lead worship, and we could hardly do without them. But clergy are particularly trained, formed, and ordained to uphold Scripture and tradition in the service of sacred worship.

Sunday morning worship is still the primary time that most lay people see and interact with clergy. We may have Wednesday night Bible study or Saturday morning work days, but the vast majority of the congregation is usually only gathered for the weekly liturgy. Often enough in today's world, it is not even every Sunday that the majority are gathered[15].

Sunday morning worship requires us, as clergy, to preach and lead the service, to consecrate the Eucharist if that is our tradition, to gather the congregation's prayers, needs and petitions and offer them to God on their behalf. It is not, in and of itself, a performance, but it does require us to speak, sing, and pray publicly.

There is an aspect of this part of our vocation that puts us in the public space, in the public eye. It is sometimes hard to acknowledge this, but we are in fact representing the whole church, and in some ways even standing in Jesus' place when we are in front of a congregation on Sunday morning.

We would never compare ourselves to the Lord, yet, as Jesus is fully human and fully God, the Incarnational aspect of what we do as clergy is extremely important. Jesus took flesh and dwelt among us, and so we, too, understand that the embodiment of our worship and our sacraments is an integral part of our proclamation of Christian belief. Thus, we as clergy say the words that Jesus said to his disciples at the Last Supper ("this is my body; this is my blood"), and we offer forgiveness of sins directly, as Jesus did in his ministry. We also wear robes and other vestments meant to hide our unique characteristics as individuals, because this helps us and the congregation remember that even when we say these words and offer these actions, we are doing so not in our own names, but in the name of the Lord. Thus we are engaged in Incarnational words and gestures, but also not confusing ourselves with God, or daring to speak for God (instead, we use the words that Jesus said directly).

This is a very important aspect of clergy ministry. It is not just that we know how to lead services, administer sacraments, and preach. It is that we have been ordained - upheld by the people of the church and the Holy Spirit - to stand in the spiritual places that Jesus stood in, to say the words that Jesus said to us, and still says to us. In this way we are the vessels of the beliefs and traditions of the church, carried with us bodily, from the moment Jesus put his hands on Peter and gave him the keys to the Kingdom (Matthew 16:19) until today, from one hand to another. Thus, even though lay people can and do assist with worship in a variety of valuable ways, clergy ministry is crucial to worship theologically.

The public proclamation of God's Kingdom and worship of God's name is a powerful presence in the world, and clergy are a necessary part of this. In the Episcopal and other traditions, priests are specifically ordained to represent the people in general as a living embodiment of the prayers, praise, and petitions of the community, and to express that in ceremony. This is a sign of our belief, our faith, and our acknowledgment of God's power and presence among us.

Clergy might do *everything*, but we don't do *anything*

Sometimes people question me when I refer to being a priest as a 'job'. Because the work of clergy is literally sacred, it can seem almost trivializing to call our vocation and ministry a 'job', as if it is for nothing more than paying the bills. And yet, I do see being a priest as my job, and not only because I do expect to be paid for it. I also understand it as my work to do in the world, in the sense that we all have specific things meant for us to offer in the world, and this is my offering. Yes, it is a holy calling, yes I do treat it with reverence, and yes I would do it even if I didn't get paid for doing it (although I am glad I do get paid!). And along with all of these things are the specific tasks that require my attention, my talents and my gifts, for which I have been educated and trained and by which I have learned and continue to learn how to make the world a better place.

What we are called to do as clergy is not really *everything*, at least in the sense of whatever comes through the door of the church, or lands on our desk because as the only full or part-time employee, we are the only ones around to do it. To allow this is to devalue the work we are called to do, and to devalue the work of others who are called to be doing these things. It is also to allow some tasks to be done that maybe don't need to be done by anyone anymore.

On the other hand, everything we do, no matter how mundane, is done by us as an act of ministry. That is, because of our particular calling and ordination, it is really impossible to separate who we are with what we do. We are not 'sometimes' loving and serving the people of God, we are always loving and serving the people of God, no matter what we are doing. So in this sense priests are doing 'everything'.

Even though this seems like a paradox, within these two statements is the toolbox for our discernment. As clergy, it is crucially important that we ask ourselves, and ask God, whether particular tasks are part of our ministry or not, using our ordination vows as guides.

When we are faced with the question, "does this need an ordained person to do it?" we can ask ourselves, specifically, how it is related to the foundation of what we are set apart to do. Does this job share Good News and/equip disciples for ministry? Does it involve specifically teaching and sharing the Christian faith? Does it foster community and serve those in need? Is it happening in church, specifically in worship on Sunday morning? If the answer to any of these questions is 'yes', it is probably a good bet that it either requires an ordained person or ordination would be a good idea (again, not always, but in the general sense of discernment). If the answer is 'no' to all of them, then we probably shouldn't be using our gifts and talents (and the resources of the congregation, or whoever else is paying us) to do this, and we may want to ask ourselves if it is ministry at all.

It is crucial that we keep our true calling, and its worth, at the forefront of our minds as clergy. The world is in desperate need of the very things we are trained and qualified to do. And the very things that presumably bring us joy and led us to this vocation are the things that we need to be doing for the sake of our own souls. And beyond these things, we believe it is God who is calling us to this work, and God who needs us to do it. This makes our life's work particularly valuable, in earthly and heavenly ways.

Being a Free Range Priest means embracing the importance of what we do and then considering how and where we do it. The obvious answer is, 'in church.' But what if there are more answers than that? Using these discernment guidelines can help us determine other places and contexts for our ministry. They can also help us remember our true place within congregational ministry. And they can help us see that priestly work takes place in all of the above. That instead of doing *everything* in one place, we can do *something* very specific and important in many.

2. The Model of Church

We may not always know what a priest does, but we do know where a priest works. "Church" is pretty much ingrained in our minds, as a place and an institution. Even though the work of the church as a whole melds pretty well with the work of clergy - sharing good news, forming disciples, caring for those in need, opposing injustice - how and where that work happens is generally a very specific model that has few exceptions. When we think of "church," we have an ideal, and that is where most of our ideas about it start.

Being a Free Range Priest is about ordained ministry within and beyond the congregation. As with the idea of what a priest does, though, before we go beyond the congregation, it may be good to consider the *within* part. Because "church" and what happens in it is so well-known, this may not seem necessary. But with the number of people who practice the Christian faith dwindling so dramatically, it might be good to remind ourselves that this model is assumed by those of certain generations and inclinations only.

This reminds me of a time when I had lunch with a bright young woman who knew nothing - I mean literally, nothing at all - about church, and how shocking this was to me.

For several years I served as an alumni interviewer for Georgetown University, the oldest Roman Catholic university in the country, of which I am a graduate. One year, my alma mater decided to turn the tables and do a project where they asked currently enrolled undergraduates to interview those of us who usually asked the questions. So I had a lovely lunch with a sophomore biochemistry major.

During the meal, I wore my clergy collar, and she asked me lots of questions about my job. I said things like, "as a priest, I spend a lot of time in hospitals..." and "because I am a priest, I do a lot of reading and writing." As I was speaking, the student looked a little uncomfortable, and finally she interrupted me and said, "I am so sorry, and I am sure I look incredibly ignorant saying this. But I have no idea what a priest *is*. I was not raised in any faith, and I have never been inside a house of worship in my life. I don't know what they do there. I wonder if you can explain it to me."

It is hard for me to explain my own shock at her revelation. I was happy to answer her questions, but it was difficult for me to even fathom the things that she did not know about religious belief, or even the customs and behaviors of those who practice the Christian faith. Even the idea of gathering together to pray and sing seemed foreign to her! I realized in this encounter how very out of the mainstream my life and profession really is.

It also made me think about how the idea of what church is and what we do there is in some ways so assumed (by those of us very familiar with it) and in some ways so foreign (by the increasing number of those who have no experience with it), and how this divide affects us all in ways we are not necessarily conscious of. Those of us who are "church people" spend a lot of time wondering how to bring new members through our doors, while those who are not don't even see our doors as possible destinations. This is a dilemma to church growth, and even more, to the sharing of the love of God.

For the sake of those both within and outside of the church, then, being explicit about what church *is* what it does and what it means is important. Being a Free Range Priest means living our vocation in ways that are not exclusively congregational. And it also means living our vocation in ways that support congregational ministry. Which means spending some time considering the gifts of the traditional model of church.

If I asked you to close your eyes and simply meditate on the word *church*, I bet St. Mark's would come close to whatever it is that you are imagining. First of all, it is beautiful, and in a lovely setting and fortunate location. An Episcopal Church in

Huntersville, North Carolina, it is commuting distance from Charlotte, the largest city in the state, situated on 13 pristine treed acres, on a hill, up a winding drive, off a country road. It is a tidy red brick building with beautiful stained glass and a historic cemetery adjacent to it. The former rectory and an economically-sized parish hall make up the rest of the small campus. It is the kind of place that invites you to wander around, to contemplate God's presence and worship God's power in the world. It is overseen by a rector, or head priest, who is both deeply spiritual and infectiously energetic, the kind of clergyperson any congregation would feel lucky to have.

For generations, St. Mark's was a congregation of 12 original families and their neighbors. According to their rector, the Rev. Sarah Hollar, it was started "by disenchanted Calvinists who wanted to dance on Saturday nights and acknowledge God's power and mercy on Sunday mornings without undue condemnation." Today it serves a few of those early families but most members are transplants to the area, a booming metropolis that has been one of the fastest growing places in the country for the last few years. St. Mark's is in the enviable position of having too many people for their building space at this time, and they have been in discernment about whether to take on the challenge of building new space. St. Mark's, in almost every way, embodies the model of "church" that has dominated mainline Christian congregations for the past several decades.

This model is so assumed by those of us who know it that it is hard to describe, because it seems so basic and obvious. But I will try: the traditional church model is a building, a congregation, and a clergy person (sometimes more than one of any one of these things, but for simplicity's sake, let's start here). And these three parts of the model work together in specific ways.

Each church has a building (or some type of gathering space), it has a congregation that gathers on Sunday - and often other times. The congregation cares for and maintains the building, and the programs, classes and other ministry that happens in the building or outside of it in their name. The congregation and the building have a clergyperson, who is responsible for leading and guiding them in their ministry and faith (and sometimes in everything else).

The congregation financially supports all of this, either through pledging (tithing), through endowment funds from parishioners past, or both. The building, congregation, and clergy all belong to each other - they are primarily responsible to and for each other. The building is used mostly (or exclusively) for the church and its ministry; parishioners are members of this particular church and for the most part attend worship and functions at this place only. The clergyperson does work only for this congregation, in this building. If they serve elsewhere or for someone else, it is either an exception or a remote ministry of this congregation. Each individual church is its own, fairly closed, system of ministry. When we want to expand, we basically start a new self-contained system of the same model (how often we actually do this is discussed in Chapter 7). This model works so well that it is really hard to think about church in any other way.

One of the reasons I became a Free Range Priest is because this model of church is so fixed in our communal mind that we have trouble changing it in any significant way, or even thinking about *how* we might change it. Before we try doing that, though, I would like to focus on how this model does *not* need to be changed. Despite the decline we are seeing in mainline Christian congregations, there are still thousands of faithful communities bringing the Gospel to the world every day, which amounts to millions of people spending time, energy, and money in the service of following Jesus.

So just like asking what clergy do, and how important it is that we remember and focus on our work, it is also important to spend some time focusing on how we "do" church, how we think about church, and how it happens. The difference congregations make in the world. St. Mark's, the church on the hill, is an excellent example, and not just because they are a wonderful community of faith (though they are). They are also far from unique - St. Mark's embodies the example of the church model because there are so many other congregations that are like them in many ways. Who do what churches do in the best possible way.

Bearing witness to God's presence

When I used to work with congregations, one question I learned to ask was "What would be lost in this community if this church disappeared?" In other words, what value does this church add to the neighborhood, town or city? What does it matter that this particular congregation meets and prays and worships God here? As we talk about the traditional congregational model, I think it is important to focus on why it does matter so much to the world.

I asked the Rev. Sarah Hollar about the specific gifts St. Mark's brings to the world around it, and this is how she replied:

"We are open and offer space to folks who a need reasonably priced or free place to do good in this part of God's vineyard," she said. "We welcome with ease people who find their way to our hill: transplants, newcomers, widows, single dads, young couples, you come to us, you won't leave ignored.

"We make a really good first impression. We get the difference between being disciples of Jesus and being 1989 churchgoers (we don't always prefer the former but we do know the difference). We are getting better and better at being Christian friends with people we don't know and people who seem unlike us and with needs we don't share.

"We are less and less about cutting outreach checks and more and more about standing with God's beloved. We are willing to ask some hard questions about our faith and our commitment to God and God's people. We are not complacent in a hurting befuddled world. We laugh a lot. We still dance on Saturday nights and gather for God's blessing and reasonable sanction on Sundays."

In so many ways, St. Mark's, and many other congregations, are a witness and a beacon of God's love in the world. This is such good news for those who find their way into church. It is also crucially important even for the increasing numbers of people who know the church only from afar. Simply being there, being present in the world, reminds its citizens that the Kingdom of God is at hand.

I was once working with a small church situated on a busy highway. One member said, reflecting on the location: "Thousands and thousands of people pass our building every day. Do any of them ever stop and join us for worship? Probably not.

"But do any of them see our steeple and cross and think that maybe they should join a church that is near them? Or think about God and how God loves them? Or say a prayer for themselves or others? Maybe they do.

"If one of them does one of these things than we have done some of our work."

In this way, each congregation adds inherent value to its community, simply by existing.

Of course, they do more than that. As Hollar points out, congregations usually reach out into the community in some way - offering resources, help and support, standing in solidarity with those suffering or in need. And also worshiping and celebrating within the community, often outdoors or beyond church walls. St. Mark's holds a Palm Sunday procession in the town of Huntersville, for example, and plenty of parties out on the lawn of their hill, where everyone is invited.

Congregations are also a source and resource of the Christian faith, for those who are part of the community and those who are not. Even those who don't come to church, or don't worship in this particular place, know that there is a church here, a place they can seek refuge and ask questions when and if they need to. When I served as a parish priest, it was not unusual for me to get phone calls and visits from random people who just wanted to talk, or ask questions about Christianity. Maybe they had a recent loss or trauma, or were contemplating something large in their lives. They were not members of the church - and maybe they didn't want to be - but they occasionally felt the need for some religious perspective, and so they reached out because my church happened to be convenient in some way. This is a real gift of the traditional congregational model.

Beyond this, the congregation is a place to find God. Of course, as people often say, we can pray and worship God everywhere, or anywhere. And yet there is something actually sacred about a church, a place where a group of people gather exclusively to pray and worship, a space set aside from the rest of the world. I worked at a church in New York City where we kept the doors to the sanctuary open so that anyone could come and rest in the quiet presence of God, and many people did. Whether or not anyone comes into our sanctuaries when we are not there for a service, they are still there as a haven from the world, as a symbol of the heavenly kingdom. This, too, is a gift to the larger community. There would definitely be something lost to everyone if they did not exist.

Churches have buildings

Churches in the traditional model are important to the community around them, and they are particularly important to the community that worships in them and calls them home. One of the most basic ways churches feel like home to us is that they are actual buildings, and they are usually extremely beloved. Lots of church buildings are old, lots are valuable real estate in and of themselves, lots were constructed by members of the very early congregation. Beyond this, these are the buildings that have housed a congregation's prayers, hopes, tears and joy for many years. It is impossible to calculate the value of church buildings in these terms.

Church buildings are usually a non-negotiable part of the church model. I have worked with small congregations who can no longer afford or manage the structures they own. Often, I have suggested that they consider selling the property, or sharing it with another denomination. If the congregation I am working with is just a few miles from another, larger church, I wonder aloud whether it would be possible for this group of people to worship with them, even keeping their own identity (the larger church has offered use of their chapel, for instance, where the smaller congregation could keep their name and community and just use the space). No one has ever taken me up on this. The building is simply part of who they are as a congregation, and they have no interest in losing it, or even sharing it.

I once worked with a group of three congregations, all in the same small town of no more than 2,000 people. Each congregation had about ten people who gathered for worship on Sunday, and they were situated in a triangle around town, no more than a dozen miles between any two of the buildings. As time had gone on and the congregations had dwindled and aged, none of them could really continue to exist on their own. They shared a musician and a priest, and after a while they just rotated between all three buildings, so that all 30 of them worshiped in one place, then the next and the next on successive Sundays. I pointed out to them that if they sold two of the buildings and all worshiped in just one - I suggested the one in the best physical shape - they would collectively have enough money to pay for the priest and the musician and basic upkeep on the one building for decades into the future. This seemed to me to be a very realistic plan to keep ministry going in an area where there were no other churches.

The members of the congregation listened politely and responded thoughtfully, but they were completely uninterested in making it happen. Each group was dedicated to its own worship space, and could not tolerate the idea of losing it. One member told me the story of how her grandfather literally made the bricks that became the foundation of the building. Another showed me the window that was dedicated to the life of her young son, who had died some 70 years before. To ask them to part with these buildings was to ask them to part with their history, their memories and connection to those who had come before them. It was not going to happen.

Part of understanding the traditional church model is understanding that buildings are sacred spaces, not just in the sense that they are set aside for the worship of God, but also because they are so special and important to the community that gathers there. I have found that this is true even if the building is not owned by the congregation, even if it is not particularly lovely or particularly old. Gathering together for worship over time - whether it is years or decades or centuries - makes the space beautiful and familiar and loved by this group of Christians. It is critically important to them that this building remain part of their life as a church. We can worship God anywhere, but we don't - we worship God here, in this particular space, and the space is part of the identity of the congregation that gathers here.

Thus, to talk about buildings as something churches *do*, rather than something churches *have*, is an accurate description. The building is a living part of the congregational identity, memory, and mission. Taking away a building often destroys the whole community, which is why it is resisted so strongly. Conversely, keeping a building open, even when that is a challenge, is often about preserving the soul of this outpost of God's Kingdom.

St. Mark's, as I have mentioned, is a beautiful place. It is also a place where the ancestors in the graveyard can peer in through the windows, where you can read their names from your seat. It is, like so many other churches, a sign and a symbol of God's love in the world, of the communion of saints gathered for worship, of the link between the sacred and secular, the seen and the unseen, the living and the dead. It is sacred ground in a world that needs it more than ever.

Churches have congregations

It may seem quite obvious that inside of church buildings are church people. It may not be quite so clear that those who gather in community to worship God and learn about the Christian faith are also forming bonds that in themselves carry the mission of the Gospel into the world. Congregations are laboratories and microcosms of what the church offers the larger community, and what each disciple is called to do in the other parts of their lives. It is a place where we practice being Christian brothers and sisters, in a way that very often feels literal.

We are like family.

Every congregation I have ever been a part of or worked with has used this phrase to describe themselves. Their building is their home, and they are like family to one another - there in good times and bad, there to help raise their children and bury their parents and walk with them through every stage of their lives. Congregations are people who have worshiped together every Christmas, every Easter, most Sundays, and who have shared meals and celebrations and offered each other shoulders to cry on and resources when they were needed and endless memories of lives shared. Just like family.

A member of my own family, my aunt Elaine Caimano, once told me an incredibly poignant story about her own life in a Roman Catholic congregation and her experience of them as family. She says:

"My children were in third and fifth grade of their small Catholic school when I was diagnosed with stage four breast cancer. Before I had even made a decision on who to tell and how, my children shared this life-changing event with their teachers and friends. By noon of the day after we told the kids I had received calls from each of their teachers, the principal and school nurse. By the end of the week our church/school community rallied together to support our children and my husband and I through this major challenge.

"No one said, 'let me know what I can do.' That is just a pat answer to make the speaker feel better. Not really of any use for someone whose entire life has been shaken to the core, and can't even figure out how to put one foot in front of the other.

"My church community just *did* things. They delivered a complete dinner to our home every single day for almost three months. The thought behind it was this was one area we didn't need to worry about. Mothers of other children called to *tell* me my children were being picked up after school, taken to their home, entertained, homework done, etc.

"The thought was the less time the kids spent worrying about the life changes they had no control over, the better they could continue to grow and mature. And have *fun*. It was okay for them to enjoy themselves while my husband and I spent our days at the hospital and doctors' offices. We didn't have to worry that our young children were taken care of.

"One day three women from church called and told me they were bringing over a complete birthday party for my eight-year-old son - to this day my now grown son remembers this as the best party he ever had. I barely knew these women. They were just members of the church and felt this was one way they could contribute.

"I also went through a difficult time with my personal relationship with God. Where I previously felt serene and complete after attending Mass, during that time I could not enter the church without crying. I used to sing joyously in church. Then, even hearing others sing in church sent an inner pain nothing could relieve. I felt betrayed by God.

"I was ashamed by my feelings. When I finally opened up about my feelings to others in the community I got support that I never would have thought of. Members told me others were praying enough for me. They convinced me God understood. I got letters from people telling me I was in their prayer circles. They took on my psychic pain and tried to make it better. And they did. I now have deep relationships with some people I probably would never have even met had this not happened. My husband and children and I came together and became stronger during this terrible time, most especially because of the physical and emotional support offered freely by our church family."

I offer my aunt's story here at length because it is so powerful, and because I know from experience that it is not unique. Congregations are worshiping families, they are where we learn about God by deepening our relationships with one another. They are so very often the very center of what it means to practice our Christian faith. With the building as their home base, these are people who are living their beliefs every day, and coming together for worship to be fed. Congregations are wellsprings of support and caring, stability and joy for literally millions of people across our country. It is no wonder that the word *family* describes what so many members feel about their own community.

I am sometimes surprised when I am speaking with congregations and I need to remind them that this, in and of itself, is ministry. We often talk about the ways that congregations reach out to others in need, but not as often about how creating a space where people who belong are deeply known, loved, and supported is also the work of God's Kingdom. Bringing others into this kind of community, and nurturing and fostering it in a healthy way, is part of the mission of the church. So many people, in moments big and small in their lives, have found comfort, joy and love being part of a church *family*. We may not think of this as ministry, but it surely is.

My own family attends St. Mark's, and we belong in a beautiful and complicated way. My husband and his former wife spent years as part of the congregation before they divorced and each spent time in other churches. Their children had grown up as part of the community, though, so both parents did their best to bring them to St. Mark's at alternating times in different years. It was not always easy or comfortable, but the members made way for this transition. As the years have gone on, the congregation, the rector and everyone involved have done the patient work of forgiveness, compassion and reconciliation. Today my husband and I, his children, their mother and her husband are all members of the congregation again. This is *family* - and discipleship, at its best. It is what churches do and why it matters.

Churches have programs

Being family is not all that churches do, of course. Almost every congregation I have ever known has done some kind of work caring for others outside the community. Churches feed the hungry, shelter the homeless, welcome refugees and care for children. After any kind of disaster or tragedy, churches open their doors and their wallets, they make food and they turn their sanctuaries into places for people to sleep. In quieter times they tutor students and grow community gardens and gather canned goods and host blood drives. In short, faith communities are usually very much in the business of caring for their neighbors and making the world a better place.

This is another fact that may seem obvious but is worth stopping to consider, especially during this time of decline in overall church membership and attendance: churches care for the community in very concrete ways.

It is impossible to actually calculate what this looks like in terms of people served and lives changed, but there are those who try. According to a 2012 survey conducted by Christianity Today and Brotherhood Mutual Insurance Company, 96 percent of congregations provide for physical needs in their local communities, 75 percent engage in disaster relief efforts, and 70 percent take part in international outreach efforts[16]. This is not surprising to me at all.

I was surprised, though, as I researched the effects of church outreach on the larger community and discovered an article measuring the impact one particular Philadelphia church has on its local community. Between running a school, helping people beat addiction, maintaining green spaces for the community to use, renting its space to nonprofit groups, strengthening marriages through relationship classes, assisting with job skills and suicide prevention, the estimated economic value of this congregation to the city is $476,663[17] per year. Of course that does not even begin to tally the emotional, spiritual, and relational benefit to people within and beyond the congregation.

Congregations run programs of their own, they take part in interfaith or civic programs, or the offer volunteer to programs run by other organizations. Church members spend countless hours taking care of others, and also all the time it takes to organize these programs, get people and supplies where they need to be, show up to open the doors and stay after to put everything away. Show up at almost any church at 7:00am on a Saturday and you will find someone setting up or making coffee for the soup kitchen volunteers, the men's group, the people who will soon be walking to raise money for a good cause or marching to fight against injustice.

Christian congregations are groups of people who follow Jesus, who said 'blessed are the poor,' and consistently cared for the outsiders, the sick, the friendless, the lonely. It is practically impossible to be part of a church and not feel compelled to extend our faith into concrete action. I like to say that God loves you even if you spend all your time on the couch watching TV and eating Cheetos. But once you understand that God really loves you, no matter what, the joy of this pretty much gets you off the couch and into the world to share it! Churches are where you go when you get off the couch, because they are busy being the models of Christian care in the world. If there is a need, I guarantee there is a congregation working on getting it filled in the name of Jesus.

St. Mark's supports a local middle school by filling backpacks with school supplies and paying tuitions for kids to go to summer day camp. They also heavily subsidize a preschool for Spanish-language children to get assistance with language acquisition and other skills, through volunteer hours and donations. Like many other congregations, they are a community filled with people who do unpaid, often unnoticed work taking care of others in the name of the love of God.

When we think about what might be lost if a church disappeared, we should think about all the lives changed by faithful church people everywhere.

Churches have clergy

This part seems the most obvious - the work that congregations do is often organized and overseen by clergy. Churches are the locations that most ordained ministry takes place - worship, formation in the faith, creating community, equipping disciples. Lay people are a vital part of all of this ministry, of course, but they most often learn and practice it under the direction of someone who is ordained. If you are looking for a clergyperson - to do a wedding or funeral, or to ask spiritual questions - you call a church because that's where you will find one. It is hard to imagine how or where someone might find a priest or minister that was not a church.

Congregations need clergy to be the bearers of the tradition and sacraments of the Christian faith, as we noted in Chapter 1. Clergy need congregations as well, to be the location and the context for this work to take place. This is the part of the traditional model that needs the least explanation. Although some clergy work as chaplains or professors or on an administrative level within a denomination, the vast majority of them serve a church. And congregations themselves can hardly exist without someone set apart to lead worship and teaching and overall mission and ministry, which is basically what ordination is. Often the character of the congregation is deeply influenced by that of its clergyperson, and vice versa.

The Rector of St. Mark's, the Rev. Sarah Hollar, is warm and funny, with a great laugh and an inherently invitational style. She constantly addresses her parishioners with the general title "beloveds", as in: "beloveds, it's time for church;" "beloveds, here's something important to consider about the Gospel;" "beloveds, I need your help with something," etc. She leads the congregation in worship and study, and also consistently presses them to consider what following Jesus means in their everyday lives. What difference being a disciple makes to them and to the world around them. She is spiritual teacher, coach, and cheerleader, and the congregation is inspired by her preaching and example.

It is hard to imagine St. Mark's without Sarah, or Sarah without St. Mark's.

Part of the traditional model of church is an inherent idea of stability and permanence, and this includes the idea that the head priest or pastor is around for awhile. Church is not just where ordained clergypeople work, it is where they live, sometimes literally. Although the day when clergy typically lived in housing provided by the congregation is mostly past, the idea that the clergyperson serves in a near-total capacity has not. As we mentioned in Chapter 1, part of the sense of clergy doing *everything* is the idea that they are pretty much always around the church, no matter the time or day. They come with the territory.

When I was first ordained I served at a church in New York City, where I also lived in an apartment in the building next door that was owned by the church. In the summer I was the chaplain for the summer camp run by the community center housed at the church, and the kids knew I lived on the grounds. Once when we were having 'Question and Answer' time in the chapel, one of the children asked where I slept - on the altar? One of the pews? Because he (very reasonably!) believed that I lived *in* the church. That I essentially did not exist outside of the building. When I think about how ingrained the sense that clergy come with a congregation, and vice versa, can be, his assumption is not really that surprising.

Given the nature of clergy work and the tendency to see the congregation as a family, it is not surprising that deep feelings of attachment grow between those who are ordained and the communities they serve. Congregations generally love their clergy, and clergy love them. They serve the Lord side by side, they share their faith and life journeys, they are there for births and deaths and marriages and everything in between. Clergy are privileged to share significant time with all manner of extraordinary people through congregational work, and congregations generally feel the same way about the clergy who lead them.

In my prayerbook, which is now worn with 20 years of use, I keep a few things pressed between the pages. I have a note written to me by a mentor, streaks of dirt from many graveside services, and a couple of pressed flowers from weddings. I also have a picture of a little boy, now grown, whose name I have trouble recalling. It is a school picture that he gave me one day, for no particular reason other than I was his priest. I doubt he remembers doing this, or even remembers me, and there was nothing particularly special about my relationship with him or his family. They were just part of my flock, and this is what makes the gift so significant to me - it was an ordinary occurrence in a truly extraordinary vocation.

The small moments of love that I have received and shared in my ministry are overwhelming when I consider them all together and I know I am not alone. The nature of ordained ministry is to bring the light of Christ into the midst of the people, and of course, the people return it. Church is the place where this most often happens, and so it is the site of millions of moments, large and small, of this kind care, support, and joy. It is just as hard to imagine a clergyperson without a congregation as it is the other way around.

Churches have tension

Despite all the good that congregations do, and all the ways they embody the Gospel in the world, all the worship and prayer offered by members lay and ordained, this model of church that seems so ingrained in our culture is nonetheless imperiled. Church attendance continues to decline, overall practice of the Christian faith - or any faith - continues to dwindle. People are no longer finding their way into church, no longer raising their children in the tradition. There is tension because the assumed model of what churches do and how they do it is no longer working like it once did.

When I work with congregations - big and small - who are experiencing this, the first thing they usually think is that they are doing something "wrong". Perhaps they are not welcoming enough, or bold enough in inviting new people to church. Perhaps there is a need they are not meeting in the congregation, or in the neighborhood surrounding it. Perhaps they should make more of an effort to support the youth of the congregation, or young families. Perhaps there should be a ministry fair or more stewardship education or more emphasis on our everyday spiritual practices. Whatever it is that is making the congregation feel like there is not the same energy there was in church a couple decades ago, or not the same number of people, or not the same amount of money, they usually respond by wanting to fix *something*.

When I meet with them, I tell them that I have good news and bad news. The good news is, it's not their fault. They are not alone. The tension they are feeling is not about trying harder, being more, or giving more. From what I have observed, it doesn't really matter what size a congregation is, how much they are serving outside their walls, or what their worship service is like. The shift they are feeling is things not working the way they used to. It is one thing to want to expand mission or ministry because the community feels motivated to serve God in this way. It is another to do these things in order to try and change the cultural climate. This is not happening by trying to do the same things, only bigger or better.

This is the not-so-good news: the traditional model of church is generally not working in today's world. Enough has changed in terms of people's beliefs and habits that the deep, institutional structure of how we *do* church is no longer working, and no amount of excellent ministry is going to affect this. Yes, it is true that the traditional model is working for *some* churches, in *some* places, but for many - maybe most- it is not. Not easily, anyway.

The same way of gathering people, worshiping God, sharing the faith, paying the bills, and supporting the ministry that worked decades, even centuries ago is not sufficient for full-time, full-on ministry the way it once was. It's not *what* we do, what we believe as Christians, it's *how* we do it, and *where* we do it and even how we *think* about it that is getting harder and harder to sustain. And frankly, how we *pay* for it. Trying harder to do the same things - the wonderful ministry that is valuable and changes the world - is not going to change a system that is broken.

Although this may seem like bad news, it does circle around to good news again, and more on that in Chapter 3. For now it is important to note the presence, mission and ministry of mainline Christian congregations, and how the gifts they offer should be valued. The changes we are experiencing as the church have nothing to do with congregations doing anything "wrong" - in fact, what they do is more valuable today than ever. But the tension of the shift and decline of the institutional church is still a very real thing, with very real consequences for clergy and laypeople.

Even a church as healthy and thriving as St. Mark's is not immune. The Rev. Sarah Hollar, their rector, says: "We are preaching, teaching, taking the tithe seriously as God commands. Still, yes, it is fair to say there is some tension. Why?"

Becoming a Free Range Priest is my attempt to answer this question. It is one way to re-consider the model of building/congregation/clergy and how they interact, pushing the edges of it in terms of where and how clergy work, within and outside of the congregation. Yet even when working in ministry that is not congregational, or working for more than one congregation, one important factor of Free Range Priest ministry is its support of congregational ministry.

One of my main motivations for this ministry is to find new ways of serving as clergy in order to support the old ways of being church. I believe that by relieving congregations - especially small ones - of the financial burden of supporting a full clergy salary, and focusing on the ministry tasks that clergy are called to do (instead of *everything*), Free Range Priest ministry can help traditional mainline congregations thrive as they are. And do the good work they are called to do.

When good churches doing good ministry with good clergy leadership still find themselves struggling, there has to be a new way of thinking about being church that will help us find some answers. There must be new ways to share the Gospel and also support congregations in the traditional model. In fact, there must be *many* new ways. I don't believe that clergy and congregations have to learn to do new things. I think we need to learn to do things in new ways. To do this, we need to understand how things aren't working now.

3. The Problem of Sustainability

Inevitably, the time comes in the life of every congregation when they are looking for a new clergyperson to lead them. In the Episcopal Church, this necessitates a formal search process, which usually involves surveying the congregation about what they love about their own church and what they are looking for in their next priest. All this is then rolled into a "parish profile," a booklet produced either in print or, these days, online.

I have seen many, many parish profiles over the years, having been both a candidate for clergy jobs and later, a consultant to churches looking for new clergy. And I have noticed is that every parish profile pretty much looks the same. Really.

Every profile I have ever seen has on its cover a beautiful picture of the beautiful building where they worship, usually with a smiling crowd gathered in front of it. Inside are more pictures of various members of the congregation, carefully curated to show multiple generations and as much diversity as possible. There is mention of the great outreach programs, stellar music and liturgy, and wonderful Christian education that happens in this place. Then the description usually takes a little detour into the surrounding community to show what a great place this city or town is to live. And finally, there may be a dip into the budget, to show that the parish is financially stable and thriving.

I do not point this out to be critical, but to illustrate how true it is - I do not doubt for a second that our denomination is full of wonderful congregations doing great ministry. Beyond this, though, the similarity of parish profiles also helps show how deeply ingrained the traditional church model really is, and the strain that it is under.

I have personally never seen an exception to the standard parish profile, focusing on the same kinds of ministries in the same kinds of places with the same kinds of people.

Again, this is not to say that anything is wrong with it, it is to suggest that we have a very well-set ideal of what "church" is. And it is to highlight what generally comes next.

A parish profile usually ends with a description of the next priest this congregation hopes will serve with them. Again, this description usually follows a set pattern, along the lines of seeking someone who is an excellent preacher, a kind pastor, a good teacher, often with a particular love of children. Sometimes they are looking for a good administrator or a bold community leader. But along with these attributes, most profiles mention that they are looking for someone to help them change.

For all of the stellar qualities that so many congregations possess, and all of the ministry they are already doing, inevitably they also say that are looking to grow. To bring in new families (especially with children), to change in some way. And they are looking for a new clergyperson to help them do this. I will repeat that I don't point this out as a criticism, but as a way to think about what is and is not thriving in the whole way we understand church in the world today.

Nothing says more clearly to me that our church model is under strain than the fact that all these thriving congregations are seeking change and growth.

We might stop here and consider that there is nothing wrong with growing. There is the old adage that if we are not growing we are dying. And certainly the Christian faith is inherently evangelical, so we are always seeking new members. Yet, if the model were really working, I would expect to see profiles seeking leaders to help establish a new mission, or add clergy staff, or equip disciples to begin house churches or some kind of offshoot ministry. Usually, this is not the case - it appears that the change being sought is some kind of change to help make the current ministry happen with more ease, or growth to occur to help fill the pews and the classes that currently exist, or pay for the building they are already worshiping in. Thriving ministries are looking for change in the model of church itself, the kind of change that makes it work better.

Because that's what we are mostly doing in the church today. We don't want to lose the basic model, but the strain of keeping up with it is burdening us. And so we try harder to make the basic components work better. By this I mean we get very economical and creative about how we are going to find the money to pay for this system to keep working. We look at each part of it: the buildings (can we use our space more creatively?), the congregation (can we start new ministries that will attract more members?), and especially the clergy (will they be able to lead us in this kind of change?). Along with this, though, we bump up against two difficult forces: how hard it is to look beyond the basic church model, and how much we really don't want to change.

To illustrate this, I will use an example I have made up, although in reality it is a composite at lots of different congregations and clergy I have known. In order to highlight the issues - and tension - facing the traditional church model today, let's walk with a mid-sized, stable congregation called Redeemer as they call a new priest, Father Stone (I am not saying whether Father Stone is a man or a woman, since some women do go by the title *Father*). As Father Stone settles into a church that has asked for a leader to help them change, these are the challenges faced by the whole community.

Buildings can change - but do they?

Father Stone was very attracted to the pictures of Redeemer in the parish profile, and indeed, the worship space and other buildings are extremely attractive, if a bit old. The windows are of Tiffany-era glass and the organ was built by hand. The old threadbare carpet has just been pulled up, revealing beautiful old hardwood floors. The altar is made of cool white stone, intricately carved. It is breathtaking.

The sanctuary of Redeemer was built in the 1800s, and the parish hall/office building was added in the mid-1960s, creating a warren of mismatched doors and hallways, not to mention electrical and heating/cooling systems that are not compatible with each other, making them very inefficient. There is no large open space that more than 30 or so people can gather. There are lots of classrooms but not many classes anymore. There are three offices, but only the rector and the parish administrator are around enough to need them. When someone comes to the door of the office building, they ring a bell, and it is necessary for the administrator (or the priest) to get up and walk down the hall to see who's there.

Redeemer's physical space is unwieldy but endearing and attractive. The members of the congregation are fiercely attached to these spaces, and spend much time keeping them up. Although as the community has aged, there are not as many of them as there once were who are up for a lot of physical labor. Mostly, they get by with a weekend handyman and community work days, but lately the buildings have been feeling overwhelming. It is hard to keep them clean, the energy bills are getting more expensive, routine maintenance is barely kept up with because of the expense, and there is some concern over how they would handle something really major, like the furnace going out or one of the windows breaking. This community loves this space, and gives all they can to keep it in the best working order they can afford.

Father Stone loves this space, too, and jumps right in thinking of ways to help make these buildings more efficient, physically and financially. An energy audit is planned, to see if there are ways to lower the utility bills. The insurance company is consulted to see what other improvements could be made. And then discussion begins about how Redeemer might share its space, either with another congregation or an outside group, in order to perhaps bring in a little income or at least share some of the building expenses and upkeep.

At first, Redeemer's members are excited about this. They know congregations who share their worship space with other religious communities. One small Presbyterian church nearby is also home to a Russian Orthodox congregation, which keeps an office and meets later in the day on Sunday. They also know of churches in sharing relationships with Jewish or Seventh Day Adventist groups, those who worship on days other than Sunday. Usually this works fairly well.

They also consider sharing space with outside groups. Already, their buildings are open to 12-step groups, and they consider the merits of allowing exercise classes, or those learning English as a second language, or other community groups to also use the space during the week.

But here the conversations become more difficult. Not everyone at Redeemer is open to others worshiping in their space, not even when they are not there. The building is sacred to them, in more ways than one, and there is some fear that another congregation will start to think of it as 'theirs', and then what if they want to change things?

In terms of outside groups using the space, there are two major snags in the conversation. The first is logistical - who will let them in, who will have keys to the building? Who will be sure they clean up and set up properly, or respond to them if there is a problem? The parish administrator and the building handyman are not thrilled at the prospect of having to manage these additional tasks, and frankly, neither is Father Stone.

The second issue is one of money. No one feels good charging non-profits or small volunteer groups for their use of the space. Redeemer's members feel that it is part of their ministry to offer hospitality and support to these groups, and other congregations, and that charging them anything more than the most token amount would be incompatible with that goal. But this would mean that others using the building would only add to the burden Redeemer already carries, financially and organizationally, rather than being a way to reduce some of these things.

Father Stone feels somewhat frustrated as the congregation considers and then ultimately rejects ways that the buildings could help them more easily continue the ministry they already do. Plans for discussing more ambitious projects, such as starting a coffee shop or a daycare on their site are ultimately scrapped.

Congregations can change - but do they?

Since not much new can be done with the buildings, Father Stone and the congregation focus on what they can do to expand their current ministry and bring in new members. They talk about three areas: evangelism, increasing Christian formation, and expanding their outreach programs. Everyone is excited about this, and there are small meetings planned and lots of energy for new ideas.

First they talk about evangelism, although lots of members are not comfortable with this word. They associate it with street corner preachers and those who intrude into their lives and try to convince them of a certain kind of faith.

Much discussion is had about what it would mean to invite their neighbors to church - would they go door to door? Would they send out mailings to new people moving into the area? Would they have an "invite a friend to church" day? Lots of people like these ideas, but few feel called to spearhead them.

Eventually the discussion turns to what Redeemer already does to welcome newcomers - having greeters at the door of the church on Sunday; following up with fresh-baked bread; having quarterly newcomers' dinners at the rector's house. They like these ministries, they seem to be going well, and so they decide to try and expand them and get more people involved.

Father Stone encourages them in this, and pushes them to consider something a bit more out of their comfort zone, like expanding their social media and talking more clearly about their religious beliefs with their friends and families. Members of the congregation are both interested in Father Stone's suggestions and reluctant to think they, personally, might follow through on them.

The discussion then turns to growth, and how Redeemer has had a few new families come in over the past year, and how they might attract more through offering new programs and classes, especially for children and youth. Right now there are only about ten young people who come to Sunday school, and the youth group is on hiatus. They discuss who might be recruited to be a new youth leader, but most of the likely candidates within the congregation have are either not interested, or have other pressing obligations that keep them from devoting the time to this. Various curricula are discussed, as well as Advent and Lenten programs, and everyone seems to think that these will bring in more people from the community, and hopefully help deepen the spiritual lives of those who attend. It still remains vague, though, who will plan these events or lead the classes.

Father Stone has lots of resources, and has led other such programs in the past, and offers to help recruit and train various leaders and teachers for these roles. A lot of discussion goes into the best time for classes to meet - Wednesday nights are good, but there is a question of whether their busy members will be able to make it regularly. Sunday mornings are also considered, but the question is always whether people will show up before service, or whether they will stay after worship is over. They eventually leave these questions unresolved, and basically decide to try a little of each - Wednesday evening programs and Sunday morning Bible study and Sunday school. The to-be-resuscitated youth group will presumably work out their own schedule.

Later in the year, the outreach committee meets. This is an extremely dedicated group of people, though there are not many and they are getting older. Still, they are proud of the fact that they run a food pantry every Saturday morning, where people in the community can stop by and get canned goods and staples for free. They also support a backpack program, filling them with food for children who may not have enough to eat over the weekend. In addition, they take on special projects at the holidays, collecting extra food and gifts for children at Christmas, and they keep the congregation informed about other justice issues and programs they can get involved with or give money to. Redeemer is very proud of the fact that they give 10 percent of their total budget to outreach causes.

What is hard, though, is that this small group of people tends to do all the outreach work, and the rest of the congregation feels a bit disconnected from it. No one seems to have the energy to start any new programs or take over the ones they currently do. At the meeting, there is a deep discussion about whether the congregation's main obligation is to financially support outside programs for those in need, or whether they are called to organize and staff their own outreach. Strong feelings are expressed for both of these options.

Father Stone encourages all of the above, and reminds the congregation of Jesus' commitment for the poor, which they remember in their own ministry. Plans are made to try and recruit new outreach leaders, and maybe have a special collection for outreach as part of Redeemer's annual stewardship campaign. The current outreach committee looks to Father Stone to help organize this, encourage new leadership, and identify needs in the community that they can help fill.

Clergy can change - but do they?

After serving at Redeemer for one year, almost all of the leadership of the congregation has now fallen to Father Stone. It is really hard to find enough people who have the time to plan and execute new programs, and to lead them and publicize them in the congregation, so Father Stone does all of these things. New programs are rolled out, and there is much enthusiasm at first, but eventually the same dedicated members attend them, as they have in the past. Outreach continues with mostly the same folks who have always done it, and with the same causes. The buildings remain in the same condition - not terrible, not wonderful, and the same big maintenance issues loom somewhere in the distance.

Two things begin to happen as time goes on with Father Stone as the rector of Redeemer: Father Stone gets very tired, and the congregation basically stays the same. Things are not bad - the budget is somehow always reached, even if it means that a couple of members give some big gifts, and people hear God's word and share worship and fellowship, and a few new families join the congregation and a few beloved members die. But nothing significant is changing, and the background tension remains.

Father Stone feels this, and worries that not enough is being done. And so Father Stone becomes more dedicated to cultivating leaders in the congregation, new members to join, and new programs to try, but also feels frustrated that these don't really seem to be bringing new growth to Redeemer, either spiritually or numerically. Father Stone is not alone in this kind of commitment, nor in the concern that the congregation is expecting their priest to bring change to them, or bring them some ideas that will lead to change. Dedicated lay leaders experience the same sense of being tired and the same sense of trying harder to change things, only to feel there is more work to be done.

Eventually, what really does change is everyone feels more frustration. Things are good, but the model remains the same - the buildings are taken care of, the congregation supports the ministry of Redeemer, and the priest bears the sacraments and the traditions of the church. And as much as everyone tries, the same difficulties remain with supporting this model. And since Father Stone loves the people of Redeemer, and they love their rector, and they all love God, they keep trying harder. But it does not get easier to support everything. It does not take long for all of them to wonder if they could be doing even more, and to each wonder of the other is doing enough.

This leads to some disappointment on everyone's part. Small things seem to bring outsized disappointments. Misunderstandings arise where they weren't before. A small group of people starts to wonder to one other, out loud, whether Father Stone was the right person to become Redeemer's rector. Father Stone starts to wonder about other positions in the church, mostly idly, but in a way that hasn't happened before. Everyone is vaguely worried that the initial joy of doing ministry together is fading.

The clergy work trap

Father Stone and Redeemer are fictional compilations, but the issues they face are incredibly real and pulled from my experience of real-life congregational ministry and stories I have heard from others. Congregations ask for change, clergy want to help them, but none of them are really sure what to change or how to change it. What usually ends up happening is that we try the same things harder - we basically do what we have always done, and hope to get a few more people involved, or a few new topics of interest, or a bit more money pledged. There is nothing wrong with this, but it does not change the underlying tension because it cannot change the shifting dynamics that are working against the traditional church model.

Congregations usually love their clergy, and clergy love the people we serve. And so it is very easy to just keep giving more and more of ourselves to try and make the most of our ministry and our commitments to God and our community.

But this takes a toll. Clergy wellness is a topic that is often addressed but not as often linked directly to the issue of sustaining the traditional model of church. Clergy push ourselves to make things work that are no longer working, and this often has consequences for our spiritual and physical health.

Thom Rainer, president and CEO of LifeWay Christian Resources, has a blog (thomrainer.com) in which he discusses the ins and outs of life in the parish, and the work of clergy. He is particularly interested in how clergy do their work, and how much work they do. He often sits with groups of people, lay and ordained, and asks them their opinions about what clergy do, how they do it, and how much time it takes them.

On his blog, Rainer writes about one such time, when he asked some questions of a group of 12 deacons at the church where he served as head pastor. Specifically, he asked them to try and estimate how many hours, at the bare minimum, he should be working each week, and what he should be doing with those hours. The total number they came up with was 114 hours a week, minimum. This included 14 hours of prayer at the church, 18 hours of sermon preparation, 15 hours of hospital and home visits, and 18 hours of administrative functions, just to name the top four job expectations[18]. That's 16 hours a day, seven days a week. Unless it happens to be a very busy week, then presumably it is more!

As ludicrous as this sounds, this kind of heavy expectation of work hours and availability hang over the head of every congregational clergyperson I know.

None of our parishioners actually wants to see us work ourselves to death, of course. But on the other hand, everyone has an idea of what they think is most important for the clergyperson to be doing. And if the congregation numbers 100 or 1,000, or even 25, that's an awful lot of expectation. Clergy feel this burden, and feel like we are never quite doing enough, that we are not bringing the growth to our congregation's pews and souls that we should be. And as long as money is tight and numbers are flat or down, we tend to tell ourselves that we should be doing more.

I am a huge advocate for clergy taking our days off, our vacation and sabbatical time, and regularly observing Sabbath rest. But when I talk about this with my clergy friends and clients, they often laugh bitterly.

When, exactly, are we supposed to get our sermons done? In between important meetings? After the next funeral? How will we be able to miss the fundraiser for the important outreach ministry the congregation does? Or an opportunity to meet new members? Or a chance to get the church's name in the media by writing a blog or an editorial?

Congregations have expectations for clergy, and clergy aim to meet those expectations, or even exceed them. Clergy do this for the love of our work, the love of the people we serve, the love of God. But it is killing those of us who struggle to do all this work, pretty much on our own.

It is something of a rueful badge of honor, clergy working all the time. It is a dark joke, and it is taking its toll. For one thing, as a group, our health is not good. The Clergy Health Initiative at Duke University Divinity School studies the physical and mental health of mostly Methodist clergy, but also more broadly. They found is that at one time, ordained clergy lived longer than most other white-collar professionals, but that this is no longer true. And even when it was true, clergy tended to suffer from more stress-related deaths such as coronary disease and diabetes, (although the good news is that clergy tend to suffer fewer accidents, suicides and syphilis-related deaths).

Today, clergy are particularly at risk for obesity, and the diseases that result from this. A 2010 study of 95 percent of the Methodist clergy in the state of North Carolina found that they had an obesity rate 11 percent higher than the general population, even after demographic adjustment[19].

Physical health is not the only measure of health, of course, and clergy also struggle with other ways to take care of ourselves. A Presbyterian study of transition from seminary to ordained ministry found that 90 percent of clergy are concerned about some significant area of wellness, most especially our level of exercise, financial savings, weight, and prayer habits[20]. The demands of the vocation, and the relatively low pay for the amount of time and skill required for congregational ministry, are taking their toll on our health and well-being.

As clergy, we tend to take care of ourselves last. Beyond our congregational duties and our own spiritual, emotional and physical health, we have the needs of our families, friends and loved ones to consider. We don't take enough time to pray and we long for more time for ourselves and everyone else. Clergy are trapped in the same system that is burdening congregations, and it is taking its toll on us all.

Why is this so? Why are we doing *everything* and working all the time?

Some of it is, we don't know what the job entails anymore, because we are so busy trying to keep the church moving forward. We can't, or we don't, focus on the spiritual aspects of our calling as much as we focus on the practical ones. Sometimes, we are working more than one job to pay our bills, because the congregation cannot truly afford to pay us a full-time salary. But we are still working full-time hours, because we love our church. Sometimes we are working so hard because we don't want to lose our job and we don't want to disappoint he congregation we serve, or neglect their needs. Sometimes we really need another clergy person (or another lay staff person, or more than one of these) but we know the church cannot afford it.

Clergy overwork and burnout are more of a systematic problem than anyone's fault. In addition to all of the stresses already mentioned, there are also geographical challenges. Most clergy, like most Americans, live in urban areas. Lots of churches, especially small ones, are in rural areas. This leads to fewer available jobs for most clergy, and at the same time, lots of churches with no clergy coverage at all. Clergy end up serving small congregations far away from where they live, and since congregations want a priest every Sunday, even part-time work becomes two full-time jobs, at very low pay! Clergy do not want to leave their churches or vocations, but they literally cannot afford to stay.

But mostly, I think, clergy are exhausted and overworked because the system is no longer working, and we can't change it. No matter how many initiatives we start, members of our congregation do not have more time in their schedules to attend, much less lead, them. No matter how passionate we are about the Gospel, the culture has changed so much that most people are not heading to church on Sunday. No matter how much we focus on Jesus' words about money, and about what really matters, we cannot ignore our own bills, our own need to support ourselves and our families, and the needs of a congregation that also has to pay for things.

This is a trap.

We know all these things, and yet, as clergy, as faithful congregational ministers, we don't know how to change the system, and so we work harder within it. It is not all grim drudgery - most of us love what we do! But we gradually take on the stress of the big picture no longer working - our buildings are still getting older, our congregations are still getting smaller, things are still not quite working and we cannot see a way of making it better.

We know we must take care of our own spiritual, physical, emotional health. We must pray. We must take days off. But most of the time, we do not see how to do this. If we do not find our way out of this trap, we will lose our health, we will burn out, we will move away from the very vocation we love so much. This tension is present in almost every clergyperson I know, to some degree. This is why I am so convinced it is not just about what individual clergy or congregations do, but how we recognize that what is happening is part of a deep systematic change, and how we respond to it.

We don't want change and we don't want death

Along with clergy health, another part of this system changing is the degree to which congregations really do not want to change. As with so many things, it is one thing to want to see the results of change - more resources, more people gathered to worship and share ministry, more young faces in the pews, more faces that don't all look the same, etc. It is quite another to have to let go of cherished traditions in order to actually change something.

One example I often use is changing the time of the service. Perhaps the 11 a.m. service is no longer attracting new people or families because it is too close to lunch, and other things that people need to do during their day. Perhaps the Saturday night service is putting undue strain on the clergyperson being able to spend time with their family. There might be very good reason to change the time of a service, or to eliminate one or start a new one. But it is very hard to make this happen, and I have never known it to happen without some resistance.

Change is hard.

It is particularly hard for people dedicated to the traditional church model. After all, when you think about it, those who are still in our church's pews are by definition the very people for whom this system works the best. To ask them to change is to ask much! This is one of those perspectives that is sometimes hard to consider because it contains things that feel obvious - congregations want new people to join them so that they might grow and change. And so, by definition, they are hoping to seek people who are not like them, who will help them become something they are not. They try to be open to things they really don't want to do, which is really hard. It is almost impossible, I think, to both hold to the traditional way of doing things and open to have it be different at the same time.

This is not just my observation. According to the Episcopal Church's 2014 statistics, when asked about their own characteristics, only 17 percent of congregations said they were willing to change to meet new challenges; only 12 percent said they help transform adults into followers of Christ[21]. By far the most important characteristic in congregations is "being a warm and caring community[22]." Being like *family*. This is a value that congregations have and that they share. Asking them to change this is asking them to change one of the primary gifts of their very being.

This is something we should all pay attention to. It seems extremely clear that congregations put huge value on feeling accepted, loved, and supported by their church community. This is a wonderful thing. And if we are asking ourselves to change at the same time, it is in some ways putting us at odds with this value. It seems obvious, over time, that the stability and warmth that congregations provide for their members is generally more important than risking it to be radically more welcoming to others who may change things too much.

This is a challenge of calling our congregations *family* - basically, family is a form of stability, of tradition, of comfort. These are all good things. Family also has very high boundaries for entrance - one is born, or adopted, or marries into one. To gain entrance into a family is a process, and only relatively few ever join. It is a pretty closed system.

When a family faces challenges, there can also be conflict, especially when bringing new members in and having things become less comfortable because new people change things. It is crucially important for congregations to explore this dynamic in terms of their ongoing community life.

This is not easy, and frankly, I think most congregations are not even consciously aware of this conflict, much less equipped to deal with it. As clergy, though, it is important that we see and understand it.

Congregations call us to serve with them, in hopes that we will help them change. But the truth about change is that most of the time we are eager to see the results but not so eager to walk the path that gets us there.

To have the kind of change that results in more money in the bank and more people in the pews, most congregations today would have to undergo the kind of radical move - sharing or selling their property, relocating to a more populated area, making evangelism a top priority for every member - that they are simply not prepared to make.

When I used to meet with congregations and ask them about their ministry, they would inevitably say they wanted to grow. When I asked them why, they would usually answer reflexively: "We need more people to help us with the work of running the parish!" Sometimes, they would say directly that they needed more money to pay for clergy and building upkeep. This, to me, is more about a fear of dying than it is about really being called by God to grow disciples and share the Gospel more broadly.

This is also completely understandable - congregations are also feeling tension. They do not want to lose what it is they have: a strong, stable, loving community that worships together, takes care of one another, and shares the love of God with others. This is not a call for congregations to change, it is a recognition of how hard it is for congregations *to* change. And of how hard it is for clergy to help them change.

What if we stop trying to change?

Even thriving congregations like St. Mark's Episcopal Church in Huntersville are not immune to the systematic challenges of trying to change. Their rector, the Rev. Sarah Hollar, puts the challenge like this: "St. Mark's is living in the tension that the mission we address - knowing Christ and making him known - is mighty and transformational but is not internalized as synonymous with ever present- church participation and support." And in this, she points out another inherent conflict for both congregations and clergy - the maintenance of a religious communities' space and institutional needs and the support of its mission.

St. Mark's has the resources and leadership to recognize and address this tension and to consider how to focus more energy on its mission and less on concerns about maintenance. But this doesn't mean the tension isn't there, and it doesn't mean that the clergy and the congregation aren't feeling it. It just means that they may have more leeway in addressing it than other communities do. Often enough, when it is not addressed directly, this kind of tension can come between a clergyperson and the congregation.

So what ends up *changing*, time and again, in the life of the church, is clergy leadership. Of course, no priest or minister stays with a congregation forever. But when we start our search process, and ask for a clergyperson to help us change - - and that person comes and tries to do just that, and then things don't change, or don't change enough, inevitably we are disappointed. The congregation starts thinking about their next clergy leader; the clergyperson is starts thinking about their next congregation or other ministry position. Even if we are all healthy and love one another, the thought of a fresh start looms when things are not going as planned. There must be something else that can be done, someone else who can help us to do it.

There is evidence for this cycle in the number of years that clergy stay in congregations. In the Episcopal Church, the average tenure of a rector, or head priest, is about five years[23]. That's the average, so while some stay much longer, many stay for much less time. And of course, there are probably many reasons for this, including that clergy leave for new opportunities or because of family needs, etc. But it is safe to assume that if everything was working very well and ministry was thriving everywhere, priests would be staying longer.

This cycle is not a full explanation, but it points to the same tension for congregations and clergy that we have been exploring here. This is simply another window into what is really happening, deep down, with the traditional church model: we know we have to change, because things are not working the way they used to. But we are not sure what to change, or how, and so we have a hard time doing so.

I am starting to think that we should stop trying to change!

I am serious when I say this. Clergy are called to very specific work, and are usually called to this work with a great deal of love and passion. Congregations are basically stable, faithful groups of people devoted to their lives of worship and service. The biggest issue that mainstream congregations and clergy face is that the system of how we do church is struggling - buildings and groups of people must be maintained, and also support the clergy who are supporting them - and we cannot really find a way to change this without closing churches and losing clergy jobs, and no one really wants to do that. And so we live in this tension without knowing what to do about it.

That's how Free Range Priest ministry was born - to find more ways for clergy to serve in ministry besides working for congregations, so we can support ourselves, and not financially overburden churches. The hope is that this might ease the tension of the traditional church model, support the traditional congregations already in existence, and help to really expand the church in new ways.

The Free Range Priest

Some clergy are called to congregational ministry, and that is where they should stay, and thrive, and be supported. Some lay people, probably most, are called to congregational life, and that should be maintained as well as we can do so, for as long as we are able to do so. Some clergy, and some lay people, may be called to ministry that both supports this model and is able to serve and expand the church around it.

As a Free Range Priest, I am just like any other priest (or *minister*, *pastor*, etc.): I am seminary-educated and congregationally-trained. I have served in several areas of the country, in big places and small, and on a bishop's staff. I am fully accountable to the authority structures of my local diocese and to the larger Episcopal Church.

The only way I am really different is that I do not receive a salary from one congregation or institution.

I help out at many different congregations as they need priestly ministry; I counsel and talk with other clergy and denominational leaders; I teach and coach Christian faith and practices, online and in person; I write and speak with those who are new to the Christian faith, or not Christian at all, but just curious about it. I get paid by the hour from lots of different locations, so I can support myself and my ministry, and I can help out at churches at an affordable rate. This does require a re-thinking of the relationship between clergy and congregation, but it also means that congregations, particularly small ones, can get clergy leadership on Sunday mornings - and other times - and still stay alive. It means larger congregations can get an extra hand without adding extra staff. And it means I am free - and motivated - to be more evangelical in my ministry, sharing the Gospel in places I might not if I were in congregational ministry.

Free Range Priest is one way to re-think the traditional model of church while still supporting it. It is not intended to replace congregational ministry, but I think of it as a vital supplement to it, for clergy and congregations. It is one possible way for clergy to be who we are called to be, and to get paid for that, in ways that support new kinds of church models in the world, and still supports the traditional churches.

Congregations want clergy to help them change, but clergy don't really know how and congregations don't really want to. I believe that if clergy really focus on what they do know - how to bear the sacraments and traditions of the Christian faith into communities - then they will, and they do, build faithful congregations. Congregations can focus on what they do best - building up the Kingdom of God by becoming the disciples they are called to be and bringing good news both outside and inside the church doors.

And together we can re-think whether every congregational/clergy relationship needs to be full-time and salaried. Maybe some congregations need only very part-time ordained ministry. Maybe some congregational clergy need occasional help from a colleague, but not year-round. Maybe some clergy fulfill their ministry by being with two or more congregations at once, or not at all, and their ministry is entirely online or in other contexts.

Small churches may never get larger, and may never want to, or have to. Medium-sized and larger churches may be able to ease the tension of wondering if they can afford everything they are currently doing. And more of us may be able to reach beyond the congregation and into the world as evangelists. Free Range Priest ministry isn't *the* answer, but it could be one answer to how clergy live out their vocations and support congregations. The rest of this book talks about how. But first we need to talk about one more hard thing - money.

4. Money is the root of all ... change

I love to watch home-remodeling shows. I find it inspiring when someone can walk into a sad, neglected house, look past the terrible carpet and dingy walls and lack of natural light and say, "This place is beautiful." Only certain people can see that underneath all the years of wear, there is a basic shape and style that can be coaxed back out into a lovely place where anyone would want to live. I love the potential of it all! Even better than building a brand-new structure from scratch, home renovation values and restores the quality of what has come before, updating it in a way that is useful for modern times. It is a challenge to do this, but one well worth taking.

My work as a Free Range Priest feels like this kind of renovation - - on a spiritual and organizational level rather than based on architecture and design. But it is no less beautiful! I can see the beauty in the ways we have 'always' done church, in the traditional model, and I can see the holes in it, too. The foundation is not as firm as it once was, for sure, and not everyone appreciates the style. However, the historic features and the loving attention to detail are just not available in any other form, and the link to our past is invaluable. There is so much we can salvage and transform.

Enough with the analogy. How do we do this? One way is to look at the financial relationship between clergy and congregation. I don't mean what clergy do - we have already discussed the specific and really important work to which we are called. I really mean the opposite - focusing on what clergy are specifically needed - and getting paid - for.

When we do this, we might notice that clergy do most of their work in congregations. Yet if they focus only on what ordained clergy do, as defined in Chapter 1, it may be that not all congregations need full-time ordained ministry, especially smaller ones. Some of what makes up *everything* in a clergyperson's job description can be done by lay people. Some of it - like my adventures in cat-trapping - may not need to be done at all.

This could be good news for congregations who struggle to pay their bills, but it is not such good news for clergy who rely on a congregational salary for their livelihood. This is one way that having an honest conversation about money can be hard. But this is a regularly occurring reality in mainline Christian congregational ministry right now.

It is possible to look at this relationship shift in a way that brings us back around to good news, however.

Clergy doing what they are truly called to do can work against burnout and restore a lot of the energy and joy of true vocation. And if a clergyperson is not needed full-time in a congregation, then it is possible they can work in more than one congregation, which extends their ministry to another church or churches that otherwise may not have any at all. And clergy working in ministry that takes place outside the congregation have the opportunity to reach those who are not interested in church but still seeking God, which is good news for all of us.

To get down to the basics of how this might happen, though, is a lot like those remodeling shows on TV - we have to focus on what goes and what stays. And because our resources are not endless, we have to talk about money.

Deep down, so much of what is happening in the church right now is about not being able to afford to continue to do things as they have always been done. This includes the part of the traditional model that assumes congregations alone financially support the building, the ministry, and the clergyperson's salary and benefits. It includes the idea that the clergyperson "belongs" to a congregation, in that they are financially dependent upon this community, and therefore available to it at all times, and for *everything*. And it includes the discomfort of talking about our ordained ministry as a 'job' in addition to a vocation, and a set of skills and gifts for which we need and deserve to get paid.

It can seem odd, and is often fraught with anxiety, to even think of our sacred profession in terms of salary and benefits, or about church itself as any kind of business model. Religion is not primarily about making money, of course. Clergy are called by God, not motivated by money, to make the world a better place. Christians have an uneasy relationship with wealth, as we follow a Lord who has a lot to say about money and most of it is about giving it away! Yet it costs money to keep a church going, and our reluctance to discuss this can sometimes add to the difficult dynamics around it. It does say "in God we trust" right there on our money. Even when we are discussing financial things, we are discussing our faith, and often vice versa.

If we really want to examine the traditional church model and ease some of its tensions while retaining much of its value, money is in the middle of this. If we could make ministry more affordable for congregations and more lucrative for clergy, we would have much more energy and many more resources to focus on mission and ministry, not to mention far less anxiety about how we are going to pay for everything. It takes a lot of faith to rise above our fear and look clearly at how financial issues can impair the good work of the church.

Changing relationships within the traditional church model means, in many ways, changing who gets paid, and how, and for what. Considering new ways we might take on financial challenges within this model will necessarily change relationships, too. This can bring challenges, but may also bring benefits. In this chapter we will look at the role of money and conflict, the dynamics of financial interdependence and ministry, and what it might mean for congregations and clergy to have more freedom and less burden financially. And mostly, we will consider how we can more openly and honestly talk about money *as* the church, and money *in* the church, as part of our communal life of faith.

Money and conflict

To begin with, when we talk about money in church, we have to talk about money that belongs to all of us as a community. This is difficult right from the start. It is an exercise in vulnerability to talk about how much is in the church budget, and how it gets spent, and who makes these decisions. Often, it is because the money comes directly from parishioners, and so we have to ask one another to give money to the church, and we have to ask for, and receive, differing amounts of money. In this, we know something of the financial habits of our neighbors, and this is deeply personal. It is also often very secretive - only a few people really know who gives what to the church. This adds a layer of awkwardness to the process. Mostly we don't know who gives what, or if others give and I don't, or vice versa. We all know that a few people have this information, but mostly we are left to speculate.

There are lots of opinions about whether or not the clergyperson knows how much parishioners give to the church. There are arguments for and against this, but overall it usually adds to the sensitive nature of how we talk about money. The congregation also usually pays the salary of the clergyperson, and the salaries or whatever staff there is at the church. Sometimes the congregation knows what those salaries are, sometimes only a handful of people in leadership knows what they are. But the clergyperson knows that their salary is dependent on what people give. All of this together adds up to a lot of conflicting feelings about money, and how it is dealt with and talked about in church. It makes open conversation about it difficult.

Lots of churches navigate this superbly, I am sure. But there are certainly those that don't, especially at a time when budgets are getting tighter, as membership ages and declines, and as building, program and staff salaries stagnate. Real conflicts can arise in congregations over how everything will get paid for, and by whom. Indeed, 77 percent of Episcopal churches reported at least some conflict within their congregation according the Episcopal Church's 2014 survey. Most of this conflict was attributed to tension over budget and finances[24].

All of this makes it even harder for congregations and clergy to have the necessary conversations about money. There is a lot of fear about whether there will be enough money for a congregation to continue its ministry as it has in the past, and what will happen if there isn't. There is also a sense of helplessness about what to do about this - will people give more? Will there be new people in the congregation? We have already discussed how congregations feel pressure to grow as a way to continue to afford their current way of being. It is hard to see how there might be another way to make the finances less tight.

Even when the budget is doing just fine, it can still be difficult to speak clearly about who gives what, who gets paid what, and how everything works together in a congregation. Even talking with our family and close friends about money can be hard - we are admitting things about our own sense of worth, power, stability, etc. To do so in community is especially risky, and an especially mature statement of our faith. Few communities are able to get to this space, and it is definitely a spiritual practice to be able to do so. It is also a strange juxtaposition between religious and secular concerns.

In some ways, churches are like businesses - we have employees and marketing strategies and maintenance contracts and the like. In other ways, churches are not at all like businesses - we believe that God will provide, that our resources are for sharing, that taking care of others is as crucial as taking care of ourselves. How we negotiate all of this is ministry in and of itself - it is discipleship in action. And like all discipleship, it requires courage and faith. Conflicts do arise when tensions are high and people have differing ideas of how to make things better. But there are ways to address our conflicts clearly, honestly, and with love.

There are spiritual and institutional challenges and benefits to having honest, open, financial discussions in the congregation. There might also be less difficulty talking about money if we had more confidence that we could, indeed, find ways forward that allowed us to not worry so much about money. And ways that allowed us, as congregations and clergy, to worry less about each other in terms of finances.

Financial Interdependence

One of the trickiest parts of the money talk is how we are financially intertwined in our life and work. Clergy need to be paid, and often rely solely on the congregation to support them. Congregations have finite resources and concerns about how they are going to afford everything their ministry requires, including their clergy. Beyond this, congregations and clergy mostly care very deeply for each other. Thus, clergy don't want to overly burden their congregations with their own needs, and congregations don't want to see their clergy underpaid. This leads to complicated dynamics!

The median full-time salary for Episcopal clergy in 2014 was $74,400[25]. The average Episcopal congregation has 61 people in worship on Sunday morning[26]. Outside of congregations with large endowments, it is a stretch for many Episcopal congregations to pay for a full-time priest, especially when considering that benefits like pension and health insurance make the annual cost closer to $100,000. Indeed, according to the Episcopal Church's statistics, the average congregation spends 50 percent of their budget on staff salaries, and congregations with attendance between 76 and 125 spend 56 percent of their budget on salary[27]. Since most congregations pay only one full-time salary - the priest's - it is the clergyperson's salary that takes up most of the congregation's budget.

This makes it incredibly hard for the average congregation to do much more than pay for their priest. The deep truth is that many medium-sized congregations cannot truly afford full-time ordained ministry. Yet they don't know what to do if they can't. Part of this struggle is the fear that they will leave their clergyperson without a job, or that they might have to ask them to work for less pay. Clergy know this, and we do not want to put our congregations in this stressful position, and so we often do work for less. Or we do the work of others, like administrators or facilities managers, that needs to be done but the congregation can't pay others for. This becomes another way that clergy do *everything*.

In this situation, clergy are not truly free to sit with a congregation and wonder what God is saying to them in this, primarily because we are not disinterested in the outcome. Our own needs are often in conflict with what may be best for the congregation. At the same time, congregations fear that without full-time clergy leadership, they will truly struggle to continue with programs, outreach, Christian formation and worship. So congregations are also reluctant to consider losing any amount of their clergyperson's time.

There are so many examples of this, though congregations and clergy are understandably reluctant to talk about it. I will use one with names and some details changed because of the sensitive feelings involved, although this is a real situation. I have a friend, "Alex," who is the solo priest of a congregation. She is also the single mother of two children with special needs, who attend a very good school nearby. Alex's mother, who is retired, lives with them and helps with the children. The congregation pays her for full-time ministry, though it is a stretch, because their membership is stable but not large, about 80 on a Sunday. In fact, they have had trouble balancing their budget for a few years now, and have done so by borrowing small amounts from an endowment. They are not sure how long they can continue doing this.

Each year, at budget time, Alex and the congregation approach this dilemma again. They have tried various stewardship approaches, but their income has remained pretty much the same for the last decade, while expenses have slowly ticked up. The congregation does not want to lose Alex - she is an excellent priest who loves and serves them well. They are also not sure they could afford the salary of a new priest, as Alex makes somewhat less than the average clergyperson of her experience, because she knows they are stretching for what they pay her.

Alex also does not want to leave her congregation - she loves them and is devoted to serving God with them. In addition, there is only one Episcopal church in her town, so if she left this position, she would have to relocate. Given the dynamics of her children's needs and her mother's help, this would be a serious strain on them all.

All of these factors make is very hard for Alex and her congregation to speak to each other with honesty and vulnerability about money. They are all aware of the tensions and trade offs that they have to make. There is a certain sense of guilt on all sides that they cannot make things better, even as they try. There is also the sense of inevitability - that someday they will have no choice but to make hard decisions, because the endowment will run out of money, or Alex will absolutely need to make more money or because of any number of unforeseen circumstances. Even though everyone has the best of intentions, they are afraid to speak freely for fear of causing pain to one another, and because they are not sure how to resolve the financial issues before them.

There is another way money is part of this interdependent dynamic: it never seems to be clear if clergy work *for* the congregation, or *with* it, which makes the responsibility for these conversations even more unclear. The congregation pays the clergyperson, and so, in this way, the clergyperson is an employee. But the clergyperson also leads the congregation, which makes it feel as if the congregation answers to them. And there are often denominational policies that try and clarify which areas of church life are under the ultimate authority of the clergy, and what are under congregational auspices. But this does not clear up the question of who is in charge: clergy or congregation, which leads to more confusion about where, when and how to make these kinds of difficult decisions.

We can sidestep this whole issue by saying that all leaders in a congregation, lay and ordained, share responsibility and authority for the life of the church, but this only goes so far. Eventually, for instance, the salary of the clergyperson must be discussed - who decides what will be paid, whether there will be a raise, whether the congregation can afford more? If there is a vestry, or leadership board, they usually do this work. But then who decides how the leadership positions will be filled? Usually the clergy has some influence in at least encouraging lay people to become vestry members. This is not to say there is anything improper happening, just that the dynamics are complicated. This can and does influence how congregations make financial decisions.

Another real example, with names changed: "Alfred", a priest of retirement age, works part-time for a small congregation - approximately 30 on a Sunday. Since he is technically "retired," he is receiving his pension benefits, and so the congregation does not have to pay anything into his pension fund, nor do they have to provide health insurance for him. They pay approximately $30,000 a year for what should be about 25 hours of work a week, but Alfred loves them and doesn't need additional pay, so he spends far more hours than that with the church. The truth is, the congregation can scarcely afford even the part-time salary, but what only a few people know is that Alfred 'pledges' back almost half that amount to the church budget.

Again, this is done out of love- Alfred's salary and extra hours help this congregation thrive. It also causes a couple of real issues. The first is, most members have no idea they really cannot afford Alfred's ministry. And they have no idea that once Alfred leaves the church - when he is truly ready to retire - they will not be likely to find another priest who is willing (and able) to work full-time for less than part-time pay, and no benefits. This will be a huge "sticker shock" for them. Even though this arrangement is helping them now by protecting them, it will make it harder for them to find and pay for ordained ministry in the future.

There is another problem: the congregation is financially dependent on Alfred. No one wants it to be this way, or even tries to see it this way, but it is true. If Alfred leaves, the congregation loses not just their priest, but their largest giver. This affects the relationship between them whether they want it to or not. The congregation does not want to make Alfred unhappy, so they are reluctant to criticize or even offer suggestions. They are not open to lively debate about topics or situations. A lot of this is really unconscious to a large degree, but it puts Alfred "in charge" in a way that neither he nor the congregation necessarily want.

These examples are just a few ways that it is hard to have open, honest, faithful conversation about money between congregations and the clergy whose salaries are paid by them. It is by no means impossible, and many communities are great examples of this, but it does take a lot of courage and skill. It is made harder when congregations and clergy have financial concerns. As the numbers in our pews continue to diminish, so do the numbers in our budgets, and this makes for anxiety about how congregations will pay for everything. At the same time, most clergy need their salaries and benefits in order to support ourselves and our families. These are incredibly complex challenges for a lot of mainline churches.

Both Sides of Money and Ministry

One of the financial challenges for clergy is considering whether or not we can make ends meet while serving our vocation. The process of becoming ordained in a mainline Christian denomination usually takes years of careful, faithful discernment within a community, followed by rigorous academic and practical preparation. All of this comes with a cost - usually thousands of dollars of seminary tuition and other program fees, coupled with many hours per week of learning and studying, allowing diminished time for work outside of this. It is a huge spiritual, emotional, and financial undertaking.

It is not surprising, then, to learn that student debt is a problem for clergy. A groundbreaking study from Auburn Theological Seminary, published in 2005, documents the steep rise in loan debt taken on by theological students, compared to the relatively low salaries made once they are ordained. The study is aptly titled 'The Gathering Storm[28]", and it was published over a decade ago. There is no evidence that the looming trends discovered and discussed in this study have significantly changed in that time. Many clergy start their careers already in financial stress.

Once ordained, they enter into a job market with fewer full-time ministry positions, where they are often in competition with others for good jobs. This is because of the challenging demographics in terms of where those positions are found. Most Americans - 62.7 percent, according to the 2014 Census - live in or around cities[29]. This includes clergy, their spouses and children. Most Episcopal churches are in rural areas[30], and they are more likely to be small and therefore less likely to be able to pay for full-time ministry. This holds true for other denominations as well[31].

So it is not hard to do this math - fewer and fewer church jobs are available to clergy, and clergy tend to live where it is less likely they will be able to find one. They are often unwilling or unable to re-locate to more sparsely populated areas, because of the difficulty of finding employment for their spouses (or finding a spouse if they are single!), and because the nature of rural church work makes it hard to sustain themselves or a family on the available salary. Those who do have full-time congregational employment in urban areas are often extremely reluctant to leave it, even if they are ready to do so, because they know how hard it will be to find something else. This creates a bottle-neck for new clergy looking for their first position, especially assistant priest/pastor jobs in medium or large congregations. The financial stress is real.

Clergy do not go into our profession believing we will make a lot of money, and it is hardly our motivation for doing so. However, we still need to support ourselves, and often our families, and feel strongly called to do so by sharing the good news of the Gospel and ministering to people in the church. After so much time and devotion to preparing for this service, it is disheartening to consider that we may not be able to secure well-paying, full-time employment doing so. Or if we do, that the church we work for might be struggling to pay us. It is more than disheartening, it is frightening.

At the same time, clergy are afraid we may not be able to make ends meet in other ways if we have to. We often take secular jobs on top of our ministry, but even then, unless we are also trained in another profession - as counselors, teachers, nonprofit managers, etc. - we may not be able to get good non-religious jobs with our particular training and education. Who pays for ministry outside of the church?

This is the very question Free Range Priest ministry intends to explore: What does it look like to put together a true priestly vocation while being paid for ministry outside the congregation? And in doing so, can we then afford to work for congregations at a rate they can pay, but not full-time? What kinds of ministry are people seeking, and how will they value it?

In the next two chapters, we will look at some examples of the answers to these questions, but for now my point is how important it is that we ask them. The tension for clergy overall is becoming unbearable, and it is clear that many leave the ministry because they have to in order to pay their bills. This is a tragedy on many levels, for clergy who are called, for congregations who need their ministry but cannot afford the way it is set up, and for a world that desperately needs to hear how much God loves us.

The other side of this tension is congregations that don't know what they will do if they cannot continue to afford ordained ministry. Already in the Episcopal Church, we are nearing the point where only half of our churches can afford a full-time priest[32]. Going from full to part-time ministry is often a time of reckoning for congregations. In the Diocese of North Carolina, when a congregation cannot sustain a full-time priest, they are considered a 'mission' of the Diocese rather than a self-sustaining parish. When this happens, it also brings with it a sense of whether and how the congregation will move forward into the future of its mission and ministry.

The same dynamic is present for churches that struggle to pay a part-time clergy salary. There are questions leadership - who will take care of the every day work of the church? There are also deeper questions of long-term sustainability for the congregation. How will they attract any new members or grow in their discipleship if they don't have a priest to guide them?

Part of this dynamic is the idea that congregations alone must foot the bill for all of their ministry and clergy support. As they age and decline in membership, this has become more difficult. Changing demographics are also unhelpful, as overall giving to congregations has remained relatively stable since 2003, and those with membership between 100 and 1,000 have seen the lowest increase in giving[33]. In other words, congregations who are most likely to be struggling to pay a full-time clergy salary are the very ones who are least likely to be getting more money from their members.

'Stewardship', or tithing from the membership of the congregation to cover the cost of ministry, is pretty much the sole method of financial support for many churches. Some are lucky enough to have endowments or savings accounts of some kind, but once they start using them for operating costs, the clock is ticking on how long the money will last. Very few congregations look outside their membership to support their daily expenses - renting or sharing their space, for example, or offering online classes or other ministry.

Stewardship itself is a model that needs serious re-thinking, though it is not in the scope of the this book. I bring it up here to say that it is another system that is not working as it used to, not only because of membership decline, but also because giving trends have changed over the years, and church members feel lots of financial pull towards their own needs and other ways of supporting those in need. It adds to the overall financial stress of the institutional model.

The Rev. Sarah Hollar, when talking about how this stress affects her congregation, mentions that the motivation to give to the church has also changed over the years, for the reasons above, among others.

"The income of our current parish families is sufficient to support our campus, staff, formation, care of one another and our worship experiences," she says. "It is sufficient to support our care of, our walking with, our befriending our neighbors in various forms of need. But the inclination to designate those funds to the church is missing and unlikely to change significantly across many families in the future."

This is the 'catch-22' for so many clergy and congregations right now - clergy can't work for less and congregations can't pay them more. This difficulty itself can become disheartening and paradoxically, members don't give as much as they once did. It is not surprising that this is all difficult to talk about, mostly because there are no easy answers, and the ones we usually find are not good for anyone: clergy get paid less, or work secular jobs to support their ministry; congregations pay what they cannot afford or go without clergy. Somewhere there has to be a better way.

Free Range Priest ministry is a bet that there is, and that it is already happening. Congregations and clergy are finding ways to live into - and pay for - the ministry they are being called to. This is a conversation that we don't have to be afraid to have. It does require seeing clergy and congregational mission and ministry in a new light. But it offers possibilities beyond what we already know is not working.

Separation of church and (its financial) state

There is one part of the Free Range Priest model that is a little scary at first: if clergy get paid for the ministry they do - on contract, rather than getting paid a salary - chances are they will not be in the same congregation every Sunday.

In order to make the model work financially, clergy will have to serve more than one congregation, and to do so, they will have to be available on Sunday, when they are most needed. So congregations will have to be open to not having a priest every Sunday, or at least not having the same priest (or other ordained clergyperson) every Sunday.

This is an adjustment for congregations to think about - and it is not easy for clergy, either. The ministry we do is based on relationship, so it is understandable to think the pastoral relationship will suffer if the clergy and congregation are not together every week. Congregations are concerned about what they will do when their regular priest is not with them on Sunday. They might have to have Morning Prayer if they are a sacramental church - meaning they will not be able to celebrate the Eucharist if they do not have a priest with them. And even if they are not, leading worship is a primary task of clergy, and to be without one on Sunday means a crucial part of the service is missing.

There are times, however, when having a clergyperson every other Sunday is preferable to having no clergy at all. And not all the work we do as ordained people is done on Sundays - there are ways that clergy can and do minister during the week.

I once worked with a very small congregation - they were down to about ten members, all of them well into their retirement years, and they were starting to face the prospect of closing the church. They were not happy about this, but they were not sure what other choices they had.

As I sat and listened to them, though, I heard them discuss the fact that they still had about $50,000 in the bank. I was very curious about this. Between this money, and the small amount the members gave, they could truly afford to stay open and have supply clergy, or a Free Range Priest, for years to come. Certainly they could afford to stay open for the lifetime of every member they currently had. I pointed this out, and questioned them about it.

They reasoned that what I said was true, and they could, indeed, stay open a bit longer. But it felt wrong to them that they would be running everything out - that they would, in essence, all be dying together. What of the last few? How would they handle this? God forbid only one of them survived long-term and then would be burdened with taking care of everything. They also discussed what legacy they would want to leave - how it would mean more to them to close with dignity and leave a solid history and some money to support other ministry, than to dwindle to nothing and possibly not have their story remembered at all.

I was so moved by this congregation and their work, and by the honesty with which we were able to have this conversation. I think the fact that I am a Free Range Priest made it easier. They had no worry about my future in this conversation, and so they could be free to talk of the pros and cons of closing without affecting my life and livelihood. Conversely, I did not receive a salary from them, and thus was not even unintentionally encouraging them to stay open if they did not feel so called. Even though it was likely that I would have been one of the Free Range Priests they called if they did stay open, we all knew there are plenty of other congregations I can work with. My Free Range Priest status gave us all the opportunity to discern together how God was really calling us.

This may seem like a sad story - having to close a church - but it was instead a very hopeful conversation about how to move forward without fear. I have had similar conversations with congregations that wanted to stay alive and active, and see the Free Range Priest model as an opportunity to do this. We will meet one in Chapter 7, in fact!

The point here is that new ways of thinking - like not having a priest every Sunday - may be challenging, but they also offer a bit of space into conversations about ministry and money. When we are so bound up in our fears of not having enough money to be effective in our ministry, we tend to avoid talking about it, as it all seems like bad news. When we have other options to consider - whether we choose them or not - it gives us a way to talk about what we really want and need. It gives clergy and congregations a certain amount of space and freedom to imagine ways we can live our callings and not worry so much about how we will support them.

Part of my own story is living into both the tension and the freedom inherent in the money conversation. When I was considering going Free Range, I was already serving as a Canon on a bishop's staff, a full-time position I had held for 5 years. I had never been without a full-time church salary since my ordination nearly 20 years ago. My husband and I carefully considered the financial difference it would make for me to go from making a good salary with benefits to going the experimental freelance route in my ministry which would not be profitable at all initially. At the time we had one child in college, and one getting ready to go (and one more in junior high). But we prayed and discerned together, and decided the timing was right. So we spent about six months saving a lot of what I made, and knew we would make do on my husband's salary alone.

Five months after I left my Canon job, my husband got laid off. This was not in the plans. Suddenly, we essentially had no income, and we eventually lost our health insurance (the kids were covered through their mom). It was not an easy time, though we felt blessed that we did have savings, and lots of other resources.

In those uncertain months, I truly understood the power of my call to be a Free Range Priest.

Not all clergy have spouses. Not all married clergy have spouses who work outside the home. Many, many clergy fear what would happen if they lost their church job, and many, many congregations fear not being able to pay their clergy enough. This time of transition for myself and my own family helped clarify my mission to find new ways for clergy to share our ministry, within and beyond the congregation, and new ways for congregations to afford ordained ministry.

My husband went back to work about 7 months after he got laid off. In the meantime, Free Range Priest began to bloom and grow, spiritually and financially. We are in a much more stable place in every way. Yet I will not forget what I learned during the stressful in-between time we walked through, and how important being able to move beyond fear and towards the freedom of new possibilities.

The church and the world

In some ways, talking about church and money will always be hard. There may be no way, and no reason, to change this. This might be why Jesus talks so much about money in the Gospels - we will always have an uneasy relationship between the power and security that money provides and the faith and love that religion calls us to. And the traditional church model has existed long enough for us to have lots of ways, and lots of opportunities, to share our resources and to share our feelings about this. Being a Free Range Priest or working with a Free Range Priest will not change this.

However, it will add other options to the model we usually work in now. Many congregations would still have full-time, salaried congregations, and perhaps some of them would be able to afford a Free Range Priest's ministry one or two Sundays a month, when they know they cannot afford two full-time clergy salaries. Other congregations would have an ordained minister three Sundays a month, or two. Or perhaps every Sunday, but not the same person. Free Range Priest ministry offers these options, for both congregations and clergy.

These options can open up all kinds of conversations, including what kind of ministry a congregation needs, and what kind of ministry a clergyperson is called to. I have noticed many churches try to support a variety of ministries - outreach, formation, pastoral care for members, etc. - even when they do not have the energy or the resources to support them all. Part of opening space for more conversation about money is the ability to be more specific about the work we have to do. Perhaps one local congregation can be the source for food and clothing for the homeless, and another can be the place with the after school program. And clergy can use their own skills and interests to support both. Possibilities abound.

Free Range Priest ministry is one possibility, one part of the money conversation that might help ease tensions in the traditional church model. When a clergyperson does not work full-time for a congregation, the congregation has less of a financial burden. And when a clergyperson works for more than one church, they are not putting all of their financial eggs in one congregation's basket. By not being so completely dependent on one another, the conversation may flow a little easier, it could make space for everyone to be a little more honest about what they can afford and how they can work together for God's Kingdom.

It can also offer the opportunity for clergy to explore what ministry in the larger world looks like. How we can work in a world that is seeking faith and not looking for it in church? Having a source of ministry income that is not paid by a congregation adds a dimension of freedom for both clergy and congregation. And, of course, there are evangelical benefits for all. This can support better financial options, and conversations about them.

Free Range Priest ministry is not *the* answer to these challenges - they are far too complex to have one easy solution. I think it is a way to open up the conversation, though. Being able to imagine paying some of our clergy on contract, rather than salary, would allow some freedom of thought for congregations struggling financially. It might allow them to imagine being able to afford a small number of hours of a clergyperson's time, which might be the difference between being able to stay open or not. For clergy, the idea that we might be able to make a living from ministry in various places, including a congregation (or more than one), might give us a little space to consider where and how we are called, and hope we don't have to worry about our salaries, or our congregations being able to support them.

To do this will require a bit of new thinking, and not just for congregations. One term I have heard a lot in the past year is 'entrepreneurial clergy'. There are lots of us out there exploring how to connect the secular world with the Gospel, and also how to get paid for it. In order to really open up the money conversation, we need to think about how we do this as ordained people, and how we think about our vocations as jobs. This can feel odd, even a bit crass, but it is part of recognizing the value of our work, and part of sharing good news with the increasing number of those who are not practicing the faith. It is also fun.

We live in a world that is changing rapidly, and is open to new ways of thinking like never before. We belong to an ancient religion that is very traditional in many ways. We are also fortunate enough to be in a time when new thinking about old models is happening all across established institutions: education, healthcare, politics, law, etc. New paradigms are being discovered every day, and new ways of doing old things - like making beer or farming - are happening all the time. The money conversation in other areas of life has led to all kinds of innovation, and there is no reason for the church to be an exception.

Free Range Priest is just the place to start.

5. Free Range Priest: Re-Thinking the Model

We live in the age of the startup and the "gig" economy. Going freelance, starting your own business, working flexible hours and locations and figuring out your own job description are rapidly moving from something only a few people do to the center of what it means to have a career in today's world. It seems like every business and profession is undergoing some kind of transformation as we grapple with technology, a far-flung work force and customer base, and increasing diversity of all kinds, both in terms of who is working together and how we are doing so.

And at first, it seems like thinking of ordained ministry in this same way is very far from what it was meant to be. How can I be a priest online? How do clergy freelance? Isn't the life of the church necessarily a life that involves tradition, stability, and consistently gathering the same group of people together over time? Well, yes. This is exactly how we used to think about, say, the medical profession, or the legal one. While it is still true that I go to my doctor's office for regular check-ups, it is also true that there are on-call doctors at my local hospital who are available for video consultations 24 hours a day. And as I have been starting up my own ministry, I have access to an online attorney should I have any legal questions.

Ordained ministry is really no different in this sense. Yes, when we go to church we find clergy working there. But we also find clergy online - teaching, preaching, giving advice, sharing the faith. We find clergy at coffee shops and bars, office buildings and gyms. We find them cultivating gardens and demonstrating for peace. New times bring new ways for ministry to happen in the world at large.

We may not think of practicing our faith, or our vocation, as conducive to the start up world, but it is. And there are clergy out there every day finding new ways to bring good news into the world, and get paid for it. The first step is focusing on what true ordained ministry is, and how it might exist in a different context than we are used to seeing.

Clergy as 'spiritual start-up'

Being a Free Range Priest means really looking at the innovative changes that are happening in other professions and businesses, and asking ourselves how we can make similar changes in our own vocation. It seems to me that part of this is taking what we do - and why it is important - down to its essence, and then asking ourselves if we have to do it in the way that it has always been done. It is the division between "product" and "process."

To give you an idea of what I mean, let's use one of the early 21st century's most successful businesses as an example: Airbnb. This company was founded by roommates Joe Gebbia and Brian Chesky, who could not make the rent on their San Francisco apartment. They had a great idea: give people a cheap place to stay when they were in town, renting an air mattress in their loft (hence, "air"- bnb) for much less than the cost of a hotel room. The idea caught on, and after some ups and downs, Airbnb has become a business worth $25 billion[34].

Gebbia and Chesney went into business specifically to make money, and in doing so, they looked at what they had available to them and what they could do with it. And they also started looking with new eyes, and in new ways. Not only does Airbnb upend the traditional idea of a hotel room - it is cheaper, usually, and more personal, because you are staying in someone's home - but it has also changed the way we experience travel altogether. Airbnb is much more like staying at a friend's place, and sometimes the friend is there with you. This also gives travelers a chance to see what locals see, to get tours or restaurant recommendations, as well as meet neighbors. People have even met their spouses this way[35]!

Airbnb is also helpful for the people renting out their space. Those with a nice apartment in a city or an extra room in a scenic location or an apartment above their garage can quickly and easily make some money by renting the space temporarily on Airbnb. Re-thinking who we are and what we have to offer means that we find unexpected gifts we didn't know we had.

One of the brilliant things about this model is that it takes a very basic concept - a place to stay when you travel - and looks again at how to make this happen. For a long time, there were two basic choices: a hotel room, or staying with friends or family. Airbnb combines the two, and makes something new - a place that is more familiar and less expensive than a hotel room, and more structured and boundaried than staying with friends. And of course, it is all available, and easy to find, online.

The success of Airbnb has been duplicated by all sorts of startup companies willing to look again at something very basic that they have and find new ways and venues to offer it, often cutting through a lot of complex administration to make it much easier. I am thinking of the ability we have today to publish our own books, or share our own artwork, buy and sell items, or watch anything we want on TV, anytime. All of these things are products of people taking very basic components and re-imagining the systems by which we usually get access to them.

Free Range Priests have this opportunity. We are not primarily in business to make money, though that is a component of what we do. Still, we are motivated by having something to share - Good News about the love of God - in a world hungry to hear this news, whether they know it right now or not. The traditional venue by which people do share the Gospel - a church building, where they gather primarily on Sunday morning - is not working as well as it once did. This leaves plenty of room for all Christians, and specifically clergy, to re-imagine where and how we do this.

Church start-ups are nothing new, although I will say they often try to take the old system into a new form. I am thinking of churches that meet at the bowling alley, the running trail, the homeless shelter, the city park. These are all quite innovative, and meet people in different places, literally, than the stone church in town. These church start-ups often attract people who have never gone to church. But over time, this has made no significant difference to the trend of church membership decline[36]. Even though these models have much to commend them, especially when they include ministry with the poor and/or marginalized, they still rely on the basic church model - "building" (or place to gather for worship), congregation, and salaried clergy.

As Free Range Priests we are called to something else. How are our specific gifts - prayer and leading worship and sacraments, bearing the stories and the traditions of our faith; applying Christian concepts to everyday life; bringing hope and good news to the sick, the dying, the troubled and lonely; standing against injustice - needed in new ways, by new people in new places?

One way we can think about this is to use the example of events that used to happen almost exclusively in church: weddings and funerals. Sometime over the last couple of decades, these milestones have gone from things that happened almost exclusively under the guidance and leadership of a religious person to secular affairs presided over by "officiants," often with little or no training at all, and certainly not tied to any specific religious faith or practice. Statistics, particularly on weddings, are hard to come by, but anecdotally, the number of weddings performed by friends and family of brides and grooms is on the rise, as is the number of Internet "ordinations" and short-term licenses granted to non-clergy who intend to perform weddings[37].

Similarly, funerals are more and more often led by non-clergy, either at funeral homes or other locations. And in 2015, cremations outnumbered burials for the first time in the US. According to representatives of the funeral industry, the main reason for this is decreased religiosity in the general population. When the deceased was not part of a religious group, and neither is their family, they are no longer interested in religious rites when they die[38].

This cycle continues in only one direction. As more people gather for life events that are not presided over by clergy, or located in a church, fewer and fewer people see religious grounding and authority as important, and we lose an excellent chance to connect nonbelievers to the Christian faith. I have noticed even in television shows and movies, weddings and funerals have fewer clergy leading them. So even in the broadest cultural sense, we are losing the idea that times of joy and sorrow are necessarily attended to by religious ritual, at least ritual that is clearly connected to a specific set of beliefs and practices (as opposed to "taking things" from a variety of spiritual sources that appeal).

As clergy, part of examining this trend is getting truly honest about how we have contributed to it. How often, as ordained people, do we complain about how much we *hate* doing weddings? And how often do we put up extremely high bars to having them - requiring membership in order to have a wedding at our church, or only scheduling a few weddings a year? (I will note here that I am not talking about pre-marital counseling as an expectation. This is a gift of the church to couples marrying, and interestingly, has now been transferred to something that happens in the secular world[39].)

The same can be said about funerals. I remember how reluctant I was as a parish priest to do a funeral for a non-member, or one that took place at a funeral home. Part of this, in fairness, was that as a parish priest, I felt stretched too thin to make myself available beyond everything I did in the parish each week. With both weddings and funerals, the pressure keeps increasing to make them less 'religious', and more open to secular customs. Think unity candles at weddings, secular poetry during funerals. We tend to make these concessions in the name of being 'pastoral', but at the cost of allowing the importance of our own religious rituals to be lost on those present. Once they lose their connection to the Christian faith, we can't be too surprised when they don't see a compelling reason to have clergy present at all.

Enter the Free Range Priest. As ordained clergy in a Christian denomination, we have the education and training necessary to officiate at weddings and funerals that are meaningfully tied to a tradition. We also have access to a lot of church buildings, and can probably easily negotiate with congregational clergy who are too busy or not inclined to take them on in large numbers. And we have the motivation, energy and opportunity to see officiating at a wedding or funeral as a moment of Christian invitation and formation, a place to welcome new people into the faith.

Clergy as spiritual coach

Re-claiming the officiating of weddings and funerals in the name of the Christian faith is one way to become enlightened about how far away from religious life most people in our culture have become. It used to be that even if you were not a churchgoer, you found yourself in church on occasion for various life events of your own, or of your loved ones. As these events happen more outside of church, that means more people have never been to church at all. There is no longer a culture in this country that presumes people are familiar with the basic stories of the Bible and tenets of our faith. In fact, many people who do go to church are not that familiar with what we believe as Christians, as we mentioned in Chapter 1.

Another way Free Range Priests work is by introducing the basics of our faith to individuals and working with them to engage in spiritual practice. Sort of like an athletic coach for your soul. There are spiritual directors, and spiritual coaching is something like this, but focused more on what it means, day-to-day, to be a disciple of Jesus, and what that has to do with our lives and how we live them.

This is not as unusual as it may seem. In a 2015 article in the New York Times, Elizabeth Weil wrote of how her daughter wanted a Bat Mitzvah, despite the fact that she was raised in a non-religious household. Weil is Jewish, her husband is Christian, and they decided when they married that they would not practice any faith, or raise their children in one. So she was incredibly surprised when her daughter wanted to be fully Jewish, and not sure how to accommodate her request. Weil herself had no desire to go to a traditional synagogue, and the whole family couldn't worship together. Eventually, though, they found a kind of Jewish "coach" - a person who came to their house, studied Judaism with them, and prepared their daughter for her Bat Mitzvah[40]. This rabbi was not part of a congregation. He was "free range," available to families and individuals who had questions about the Jewish faith, and willing to work with them personally.

I find the coaching idea compelling, not just because so many people are raised without any religion today. I have also noticed that when I go to church on Sunday - and I go to a different church almost every Sunday - the focus is on worship, and on those who already believe. If you were to walk into most churches, randomly, you might be given a warm welcome, you would hopefully be given a service book or bulletin, but there would be little or no instruction on the faith itself.

In the Episcopal tradition, we say the Nicene Creed each week, which outlines the beliefs of the Christian faith, but we do not go into what that means or why. And certainly, during worship is not the time to do this. But most churches do not offer much Christian education, outside of the occasional Bible study (There are lots of reasons for this, but that is another book). So it is possible to attend Christian worship every week, and never learn much about the Bible, the Christian faith, how it matters in our lives and how we are called to share it with others.

As Free Range Priests, there is a lot of room to see ourselves as Christian coaches. In many ways, church is like the gym, the place we go to gather with others like us, who believe like we do and orient their lives around the same principles. For the rest of the week, just like athletes do, we are responsible for our day-to-day 'working out', keeping ourselves healthy. And we occasionally work with a coach, who imparts their own wisdom and training on us, to help us reach our goals, and for specific training and motivation.

Coaching, in itself, is a Free Range profession. More and more athletic coaches and personal trainers are setting out on their own[41]. People are interested in caring for their bodies and setting fitness goals, and are willing to pay experts to help them. Still, it is a leap for even this kind of coach to become Free Range.

Mike Smith runs [4D Endurance](#) in Mooresville, north of Charlotte (Full disclosure: He is my husband's triathlon coach). His life's journey brought him from Canada to Florida and then to North Carolina. Most of that time his professional life revolved around IT. But he was always an excellent athlete - competing as a pro motorcycle racer, a semi-pro mountain bike racer, and a long-distance runner - and very interested in fitness.

He decided to continue his education as a fitness trainer, and gradually started working as one, even while he was still in IT. And then he transitioned into starting his own coaching business and gradually became a full-time fitness professional. Says Mike: "Starting a business really just happened organically. At my core, I have a passion to help others and also to grow. I wanted to help others achieve their goals and have something for my family which is why I started the company."

It may have started organically, but that does not mean it was easy. In fact, according to Mike, it was a huge leap of faith: "I was essentially starting all over again, with a family depending on me." Faith is our business as clergy, and if anyone understands this, we do. But I wonder how often we are called to live it, taking this kind of risk to do what we love, on a path we cannot see clearly.

I wonder too, as clergy, how often we feel this way about our ministry as a set of beliefs and practices that we can bring directly to people anywhere, at any time. If we think about our ministry as a chance to help people grow and learn in ways that will bring enormous benefit to their lives. I think the idea of ministering is often about being present with others, and about being comforting. But we are also there challenge - - challenging others to increase their spiritual fitness, and giving them the tools to do so.

When we care enough about sharing the love of God, we get bold enough to bring the practices of our faith directly into people's lives. This can happen in a congregational setting, and I am sure it does, every day. Yet with the increasing number of those around us - especially young people - who are extremely reluctant to join a church and know very little to nothing about the Christian faith, we may be called to step further outside our doors, outside our regular way of doing things. Sharing the good news of the Gospel and equipping disciples is part of what clergy are called to do, and the concept of spiritual coaching can help us consider new ways to do it.

Clergy as Teachers

Lots of clergy serve in educational roles, from elementary to seminary level. In Chapter 8 we will look at the term *bi-vocational*, and what that really means versus how we usually use it in the church. In its true sense, it literally means having more than one calling. Being ordained and a teacher is a classic example of two callings in one, and there is a long tradition of this sort of bi-vocational work. Teaching the Christian faith in particular is not just part of the work of clergy, it is very much needed in the world today. With fewer people in church, and fewer getting any kind of true understanding of the basic Christian story, it is obvious that there is a need to be filled.

Yet working within the educational system is as complicated as working in the institutional church today. Elementary and high school education is debated on so many levels that are clearly beyond the scope of this book, and my expertise. I mention it only as an area that is full of possibility for reimagining how religious instruction is brought to this age group, and how clergy might be part of that reimagination.

University and seminary level education are also places undergoing major shifts in how things are done. Tenure is harder to come by, and the system is changing. More faculty are adjunct, but this is not as stable for teaching, and generally does not pay as well[42]. Seminaries are searching for new ways to retain students, and even survive, because of church decline and because the model of three years of residential education is getting harder to sustain[43]. "Free range" teachers are in the same sort of space as Free Range Priests are - examining the core of their call and then finding new ways to reach those who need them.

All this is part of the base of Free Range Priest thinking. Education, like ministry, is something so basic that we take it for granted. Yet when it stops working like it used to, we stop and re-examine what it is there for, why it is necessary. What do we really need to learn? What are the basics, who gets to decide this, and why does it matter? Teaching and learning are crucial parts of all human community. When, where, what and how we teach and learn are constantly being discerned. We live in an era when that discernment is happening faster and more publicly, and in terms of religious education, clergy have lots of room for input, and much at stake.

Living and teaching the Christian faith is a primary role for clergy, and the shifting education system opens all sorts ways to re-think ordained ministry along with changes in education. Online teaching is exploding in popularity[44], and no matter what its drawbacks are, it is becoming a regular feature of how people learn. Theological education is no exception to this[45]. Teaching the faith on all levels - from children to adults, from the basic stories to preparation for ordination, is a huge mission field that is getting larger every day.

Some clergy are out there already.

The Rev. Chris Yaw is the rector of St. David's Episcopal Church in Southfield, MI and the founder of the online learning website ChurchNext.tv. It is primarily oriented towards congregations - educating lay people who want to learn more about the Christian faith. It offers more than 300 courses, on various levels, and is dedicated to broad theological education.

"Our vision is that every congregation can have their own online school," Yaw says, "branded that way and organized that way, giving congregations the capability of choosing from our ever-growing library, as well as giving the the ability to write, produce, and upload their own custom courses (with our help if needed). Congregations can access both our 'For Groups' format of courses (meant to be taught in a gathered group) as well as our 'For Individuals' formatted courses, which are designed for individuals to take on their own."

Yaw noticed that even dedicated members are not in church as often as they used to be, and not getting the same level of formation in the faith. So he started Church Next as an offering that fits people's lives and helps them grow as disciples. Church Next also has a subscription service for individuals who want access to their library.

"Church Next is that place between the seminary and the pew," he explains. I know of a pastor of 550 people that maybe three would take an online course from a seminary. I can double or triple that with my online school[46]."

This thinking is a classic example of taking a *product* - Christian education for congregations and individuals, and re-thinking its *process* - classes at church that take place on Sunday morning or Wednesday evening. Clergy are often concerned that church members are not getting enough formation in the faith. We are often dismayed that the classes we put together are not well-attended. We can stop there and tell ourselves that people just aren't that interested in learning more about Christianity, or that we aren't good teachers, don't have good material, etc. Or we can look again at the process instead of the product.

Thinking about Christian education in mostly terms of *how* it happens rather than if it happens, or with whom, or what it contains, led Yaw to a place where a solution appeared. He changed the process to something more accessible and in this, made Christian education more available to many more people.

Theological education everywhere has room for this kind of thinking, and Free Range Priests are in a prime position to seek ways to implement it. From online classes to adjunct faculty to instructional methods not yet imagined, teaching the Christian faith can find new forms in new ways. We still need it - I think we need it now more than ever. The *product* is incredibly valuable. The *process* is wide open in today's world.

Clergy as Freelancers

Lots of us have great ideas about how to make the church better, and how to share the Gospel in new ways. Most of us don't quit our day jobs to do so. As we have discussed throughout these pages, there is a great deal of fear among clergy that we won't be able to support ourselves while serving in the vocation to which we are called. Going Free Range is basically going freelance, and it is not exactly filled with job security.

Thinking of new ways to serve God and the church is not the same as thinking of new ways to get *paid* while serving God and the church. Airbnb was started by a couple of guys who needed to pay their rent, but it was still a risk. Free Range Priest was started in response to all the fear and frustration clergy feel around sharing the Gospel, serving the church, and being able to support ourselves doing both. There is risk inherent in this, too.

I will digress here to reiterate that the "free" part of Free Range refers to where and with whom we are engaged in ministry, and how we get paid. Our connection to the Christian faith, our ordination in it, and our allegiance and obedience to the established authorities that govern it, remains the same. I am an Episcopal priest in good-standing, I am under the guidance and discipline of my bishop, I am fully background-checked and have the appropriate credentials. I am engaged in the councils of my church and vested in the pension fund.

I think this is extremely important, for several reasons. First, as with all clergy, I do not dare stand on my own authority when representing God's presence in the church and in the world. I represent the authority of the followers of Jesus who have established a church over centuries, and in whose traditions I have been fully formed and guided. When I meet people who have never heard of God's love, I am bringing them not just my thoughts on the matter, but what God has revealed to God's people, as I understand it, over time.

Also, accountability is extremely important in religious community. Not just as a safeguard against inappropriate behavior, but to make sure it is the beliefs of the church that are being shared. That requires consistent feedback and discernment from a larger group, and it is part of the authority of the church. We grant it to those we ordain, and we expect it to be used wisely and shared widely. Thus, I see myself as very much a priest of the Episcopal Church, and a representative of the wider Christian community, as well as a Free Range Priest.

This is something, incidentally, that turns out to be a feature of startup life in other professions as well. Secular wedding and funeral officiants now must have some sort of credentialing before they are allowed to lead a service[47]. Coaches certainly need training and education. And those in most professions, even freelancing, are still tied to the core of what they do and why they are especially able to do it well. There is a body of knowledge and expertise that is demonstrated in some concrete manner. Maybe none of us is truly "free range" in this sense.

That being said, there is a way Free Range Priests are indeed freelancers - we look at what we are doing in terms of discrete contract work. Instead of working in one place, doing one job, we are available for different kinds of work as it comes to us. A congregation calls us for a Sunday service; a group asks us to lead a retreat; an individual seeks us out for spiritual counsel; someone downloads our book online, or takes one of our classes there. In these ways, we interact with a variety of different people, doing a variety of different things, inside and outside the congregation. This is very different from getting a salary and then being responsible to and for one particular community.

Freelancing has become a much larger part of our economy in the past few years. According to the Bureau of Labor and Statistics, there was an increase of roughly 1 million self-employed workers in this country between May 2014 and May 2015. By 2020, some estimates indicate that 40 percent of Americans will be contract workers[48]. This may not necessarily be a good thing - there is a lack of stability, for instance, and there are usually no built-in benefits. Some freelancers make less money than they would if they were drawing a salary. On the other hand, there are definite upsides: flexibility of hours, not having a commute, more creative freedom, being your own boss, and the chance to focus on the things that bring us joy rather than the things other people think we are supposed to do. The opportunity to be agents for change in our own professional sphere.

Again, in some ways it is odd to consider clergy as freelancers. Our vocation does not really lend itself to this type of work. Instead, we are focused on building relationships over time, often remaining in one place, helping to create a Christian community. So much of clergy ministry is immeasurable. It is simply about being present.

I remember well, and poignantly, a moment from my own ministry, when I was saying goodbye to one of the congregations I had served for several years. Standing at the door after that last service, one of the older members took my hand as we bid each other farewell. I had known her family very well over the years, and I had been with them through the long final illness of her husband. She cried as she said goodbye, because, as she said to me, "the new priest will never have known Richard." It brought tears to my eyes, then and now, to think of the truth of this statement and what it meant - that the priest who came after me, no matter how much they loved this family, would not truly know them in the way that I did. This helps me remember, even now, the deep importance of the work of clergy in a congregation, and how hard it is to quantify what we do.

The "free" in Free Range also does not mean that we detach ourselves from such deep spiritual relationships. There is no doubt that something will be lost if ministry does not constitute being in one place over a long period of time. I do not advocate that all ministry should be Free Range. Yet there are relationships to be gained by being in more than one place at different times, especially when those places extend outside of the church, online and in person.

Today, in fact, as I finish writing this book, I am heading out to meet a former neighbor of mine for coffee. Her elderly father is dying, and it seems he has outlived his Roman Catholic priest. The new priest is not someone he knows, because he has not been able to attend church for years due to his frail health. That priest has not had time to visit - he is overwhelmed with a very large congregation, where he is the sole pastor.

My neighbor knows I am a Free Range Priest, and she is visiting with me to discuss her father's spiritual needs as he nears the end of his life, including questions about funeral. We are just at the beginning of this process, but I expect that it will draw me into a relationship with this family, even though the time I spend with them will be proscribed and not long in duration - though we don't know how long it will be. This is just one way I am encouraged that Free Range - and freelance - can still mean true connection and true Christian community.

The "free" in Free Range means that I am available to contemplate this possibility, and this pastoral relationship, across denominations and the normal scope of congregational work. Because I do not have my own church members to tend to, I can see everyone, everywhere, as potentially belonging to my church, and they can see me as their priest. Still, there is quite the leap between being available for such work and making a living doing it. This is where the freelance dream becomes a reality, and where we can learn from those who take it on in other professions.

On our own, together

I first met Jessica Bramlett and Jessica Willingham online. In fact, I have only ever interacted with them online. Bramlett is a graphic designer who lives in Arkansas. Willingham is a copywriter/editor who lives in Wyoming. Together they started Rarest Fortune, an online business that combines their talents and brings companies a 360-degree service that helps them with website, branding, and promoting what they do. Rarest Fortune helped me launch a new website and hone the message of my ministry. I was impressed and fascinated by how well these two young women work together and grow their own business - especially when they live so far away from each other. I asked them to tell me the stories about how they decided to go out on their own.

Both Jessicas told me that they quickly found jobs in their respective industries when they graduated from college. They were grateful for the work, but fairly disillusioned by what they were assigned to do. Jessica B. said that she felt constrained creatively, as she was following others' designs and not her own. Jessica W. remarked on the way her coworkers would sometimes dismiss her ideas because she was young. At the same time, each of them were getting calls for other project work that they didn't have the time to take.

Each Jessica decided individually that it would be more productive, vocationally and financially, to just bring her gifts directly to the world. So they went out on their own before they ever met. They both joined an online community, however, designed to support women with their own businesses. They met in person at a conference for this community, and started to see how their gifts, talents, and individual clientele were very compatible. Eventually they teamed up to form Rarest Fortune, and their business is thriving.

As clergy, we are in the community business. No one has to tell us that teaming up, even when we are Free Range, is a good idea for our ministry, and for our souls. Jesus himself called disciples around him, and sent them out two-by-two to do their work in the world. Luckily for us, when we are ordained today, we are ordained into a tradition, usually a denomination, and a supportive group of fellow ministers of the Gospel. In the Episcopal Church, we are ordained by the laying on of hands by a bishop, and also the hands of every other priest who is present at the time. In addition, the bishop asks all present if they will support the ministry of the person being ordained, and the congregation responds with a hearty, "we will!" We cannot be clergy - or Christians - alone.

Yet even how our community supports us is an area for re-examination. The larger structures of denominational oversight can themselves be cumbersome in terms of supporting ministry, especially outside the congregation. It is one thing to defend the faith and set boundaries on who is ordained and for what purpose, as denominations clearly do. It is another to be able to support clergy and congregations in every way as they grow and change.

Denominational administration is undergoing the same challenges that congregational ministry is, for the same reasons. There are not as many resources as there once were, or as many people who serve. Congregations have more needs, especially financial, and clergy need to be raised up, formed and educated, and employed. Denominational leadership, like congregational leadership, is stretched to do the work it is already doing. To creatively think outside the box of traditional clergy and congregational ministry is a lot to ask on top of this.

In my first year of being a Free Range Priest, one of my biggest accomplishments was continuing to stay vested in the Episcopal Church's Pension Fund. This is not a small issue, either personally or organizationally. I have currently been ordained for 17 years, and I am extremely grateful to serve a church that protects me financially for retirement. I would very much like to continue contributing to my pension, especially as I approach the crucial twenty-year mark. Since I no longer serve on a church or diocesan staff, though, there was not an easy way to classify my ministry, how it is done or whether it even qualifies as ministry in the Episcopal Church. The structure is simply not set up to see ministry as a Free Range activity.

As I delved into this, though, I was excited to learn that in the Episcopal Church, the leadership is seriously engaged in looking at new ways of doing ministry, and new ways of supporting clergy engaged in this ministry. This includes support for retirement. With the help of my bishop, and lots of people at the Church Pension Group (CPG), I was able to get Free Range Priest recognized as a true ministry and continue to contribute to my pension.

This is good news for me, and also good news in terms of wider church administration. It is hard for organizations to change, and church organizations have a calling to support the structure already in place that is as strong, maybe stronger, than supporting innovation. This, to me, means there is room to bridge the gap. Airbnb, for example, did not supplant the hotel industry, and is not meant to. Online learning will not make in person education disappear, nor should it. And by no means will Free Range Priest ministry ever take the place of congregational, or denominational, traditional church structure.

Rather, new ways of thinking mean that new ways of ministry can exist alongside the traditional model, in ways that are hopefully supportive for all. If clergy get paid as freelancers, one place they can freelance is the congregation! Even in the larger denominational level. This might ease financial and vocational tensions, and open new venues, for everyone. At least that is the hope.

Making the leap

My friends the Jessicas found one another because they sought out professional community and found in it ways to support one another and to work together. One huge advantage we have as ordained clergy is the built-in community our church structure usually provides. And even as it supports us, it is also a space that can be open to a more Free Range point of view. This highlights one way we can recognize the core strengths of what we do and believe as clergy and how we might open our thinking about new ways to use them.

This leads back to the issue of *product* and *process*. As congregational or Free Range Priest clergy, our product is the same: the Gospel. We preach, we lead worship, we teach, we give pastoral care, we baptize and marry and bury others. The Gospel is free, of course. But our work is not!

Thinking like startups, coaches, teachers, freelancers, and even administrators are just a few examples of the planes of ministry that we can reimagine our work, and how we get paid to do it. But even after we have great ideas, there comes a time to implement them. This is when we truly go Free Range.

For several years, I had an amazing spiritual director. Tom Cushman saved my ministry many times by listening patiently with me as I struggled to hear God's voice. Frankly, he saved my life a few times, as well. The only reason he is my former spiritual director is that he is now retired, but I still call him occasionally to keep him posted on my life.

As I went from being the rector, or head priest, of my own church to serving on a church staff, I gradually became aware of the challenges facing clergy and congregations in today's traditional church model. I experienced a lot of them myself. And I kept having the feeling that I could be part of addressing and overcoming some of these challenges.

That this, in itself, could be ministry.

I kept gathering thoughts and experience, but deep inside I kept hearing the voice that said, "It is easy for you to have opinions while you also have a comfortable full-time institutional church job." I kept talking with Tom about what this meant, how I could go out on my own instead. Starting my own church would in some ways just repeat the traditional model of building/congregation/clergy, and seemed like it would face the same obstacles that others were already dealing with. I felt like there must be another way.

Eventually the day came when I was so clearly planning what this ministry would look like that I started thinking about when it should start. I agonized over a date, on my own and in conversation. Finally, Tom said, "It seems like this ship has already sailed." He was right, of course. In my mind, I was already Free Range. All I had to do was leap. And so I did.

I am hardly alone.

One of the enormous blessings of this ministry has been meeting a few of the many others who are already Free Range Priests, though they may not call themselves that (yet). One part of my own call is to highlight Free Range Priest ministry as not something that is the exception - places we might use terms like "non-parochial", "bi-vocational" or "supply". Rather, I would like to call into our consciousness all the ways that this ministry can and does expand the way we share the Gospel and make Jesus known in the world. And all the clergy who are already serving in this way, as the true call of their lives.

6. Free Range Priest in the World

Who are these Free Range Priests and what kind of work are they doing?

The vision of this ministry is clergy serving God and the church in ways and places that are sustainable and life-giving, inside and outside of the congregation. Its benefits include sharing the Gospel widely in an increasingly secular culture, clergy having the ability to support themselves spiritually and financially in a changing institutional environment, and congregations moving into the future with ordained ministry they can afford.

I know there are ways this is already happening, because I see it. Ever since I went Free Range, people want to talk to me about their own ministry. I am not surprised that I have met people all over who are doing innovative work.
I think it is part of my own call to share what I find. My hope is that by highlighting places where Free Range Priest ministry is emerging - and thriving - and serving my own priesthood by fostering and supporting it, I can help transform my own corner of God's Kingdom. As I moved forward with this work, I have met clergy already serving as Free Range Priests, although they didn't call themselves that until I introduced them to the term. This is part of the adventure for me - getting to meet others in transformational ministry, and getting to share all this vision and work happening in the world.

Clergy engaged in innovative ministry - and getting paid for it in lots of ways - are everywhere. Sometimes it is hard to see, because the idea of building/congregation/clergy is so ingrained in our collective mind as the only way that church really happens. Once I started my own ministry though, and particularly when I started writing this book, I kept meeting other Free Range Priests along the way. It's probably closer to the truth to say they kept popping up in my inbox.

I feel especially blessed to have crossed paths with Jabriel Ballentine, Lisa Cressman, and Jay McNeal. They live in different areas of the country, serve in different denominations, and have widely different stories. Yet their callings are remarkably similar. Each of them serves outside the traditional congregational model. Each of them works in a way that brings those who are already familiar with the Christian faith - and those who are not - deeper into the tradition. And while all of them support congregational ministry with their work, none of them is paid a salary to work exclusively in a church. This is Free Range Priest ministry in a nutshell, how this vision is shared in the world.

The Prophet

It all started with an email.

Hey, Father Cathie! We have a friend in common who says that we should meet.

Already I liked Fr. Jabriel Ballentine, his warm, invitational manner, and his ability to switch from small-talk to complex aspects of faith with ease. I would learn more about this eventually, but first I was intrigued about who we knew in common and why he reached out to me.

Our mutual friend is the Rev. Canon Michael Buerkel Hunn, Canon to the Presiding Bishop of the Episcopal Church, who knew I was just starting out as a Free Range Priest. In fact, Michael taught me much of what has become the base of my ministry when we served together in the Diocese of North Carolina. So when he met Jabriel, who serves on the Executive Council of the Episcopal Church, and learned of his expanding ministry, he immediately felt we should get to know each other. So we did.

Ballentine is an Episcopal priest who was born in Detroit, Michigan and raised in St. Thomas, Virgin Islands. He now resides in Florida, and at the time of our first email, he was considering leaving his job as the rector of an Episcopal Church there, destined for something new. He and I had several conversations as he transitioned from congregational ministry to his own unique way of serving his priesthood in the world.

Ballentine's life seems always to have followed a wide, eclectic path while also listening to God's call. He has worked as a consultant and communications director in the political world of Washington, DC; he has been a restauranteur, a carpenter, and a teacher of children with special needs. Along with his professional life, he has practiced his faith deeply, especially influenced by the Ethiopian Orthodox Tewahedo Church. He was raised in the Episcopal Church, though, and there he eventually returned, went to seminary, and was ordained a priest in 2012. Still, he says, he brings the "simple and profound" faith he found in Orthodox Christianity with him, as well as all his varied life experiences.

Ballentine and his family eventually settled in Orlando, and he was called to the position of rector (head priest) at a church there. But he did not feel settled or fulfilled serving a congregation in this way. "I don't presently have the patience to be a rector," he explained. "I feel called to teaching and being a companion with others as they try to find their way in life."

This is one hallmark of the Free Range Priest. Ballentine is very much a priest - called and ordained to bear the sacraments and traditions of the church. Yet this calling does not necessarily fit the job description of being a pastor to one flock, and everything this entails. Instead, he is intent on equipping disciples in their everyday lives, instilling them with practical, Gospel-based bread for their journey, whether they are currently church members or not. His vocation is the same as any other clergyperson, but how he lives it is not.

Ballentine had already begun this work while still in the congregation through his website, JahBread.com, where he posts his blog and includes his poetry, in an album called *Journey to the Promised Land*. Since he has started his own ministry, the site has expanded to offer Bible study resources, spiritual direction, relationship coaching, and thoughts on racial reconciliation.

It is these last two subjects that have drawn Ballentine further into how the practice of the Christian faith is intertwined with the most important issues of our lives. He is the author of *Game Changer: How to Find a Championship Love*, a Christian relationship advice book, which he supplements with articles, coaching, and an active Facebook page. In this he takes on one of the most basic, and often perplexing, journeys of our life - finding love - and infuses it with faithful strategy. It is a topic that applies to almost everyone, addressed in a way that is not often available in congregational life.

Ballentine also hosts a podcast called *Racial Heresy*, which he co-produces with partner Cayce Ramey. As new tensions around race and ways to address them have come to the forefront of our culture, Ballentine has responded with this frank, boundary-pushing on-air discussion. Here he is fully a prophet, speaking against injustice, bringing truth to light, and calling us all to acknowledge how following Jesus brings a call of confession, forgiveness, and reconciliation. He also models the way this works, by engaging in the kind of honest conversation that occurs only when people have deep respect and trust for one another that is born from the belief in an all-powerful, all-loving God. It is a safe space, but right on the edge.

All clergy understand there are times and places we must speak with a prophetic voice. This can be tricky, though, when we are serving a congregation. As pastor to a group of people, we must take into account their diverse spiritual needs as we seek to reach them with the truth of the Gospel. This can sometimes soften our own message out of necessity, in terms of our responsibility to our flock. A Free Range Priest like Ballentine has the ability to speak as clearly as he needs to because he does not have the same consideration. Instead, he is able to reach those who may need to hear a stronger voice, unvarnished yet delivered with love.

Ballentine's ministry is pure church, outside the congregation. It is prayerful, worship and Scripture-based, forming disciples in community, reaching out to those in need, and calling out injustice. This is what clergy do, and in this case, it happens in a context that is not traditional - online, on air, in print, in person. He is able to reach those inside and outside the faith with the Gospel in unexpected ways, with a unique, prophetic power.

The Preacher

Soon after I met Fr. Jabriel, I received another email, out of the blue.

Dear Father Cathie,

I'm the Founder and Steward of Backstory Preaching (BsP), a first-year pilot project in the Diocese of Texas. My partner is the Rev. Dr. Micah Jackson, the preaching professor at Seminary of the Southwest in Austin.

Would you be interested in having a conversation with me?

Of course I was interested. I had no idea who she was, or what she was talking about, and I only knew one person in the whole Diocese of Texas (*not* the Rev. Dr. Micah Jackson). So I was completely intrigued by how the Rev. Dr. Lisa Kraske Cressman found my email and why she wanted to talk.

It turns out we have friends in common - not through the church, as one might suspect, but a much more complicated web that stretches to my former husband, through acquaintances to Micah's wife, and all connected via Facebook (of course!). Lisa knew a bit about my own ministry, and she wanted to share some about hers. On that day we unknowingly began a friendship and a professional partnership. But first I came to understand her call, vision, and how she is a Free Range Priest.

Cressman exudes strength and gentleness in a way that makes you want to become a little bit more of both. She also has one of those remarkable stories of how the Holy Spirit can chase you all over the place. Although she lives and serves in Houston now, she is from Minnesota, and has also lived in Wisconsin, Utah, California and Indiana. She studied, trained and served as an intensive care nurse before hearing the call to ordained ministry, going to seminary, and becoming a priest.

Cressman spent a decade in parish ministry and offering spiritual direction, and another decade preaching regularly as a non-stipendiary (unpaid) priest while raising her children. Then her husband was offered his dream job in Texas, the family relocated, and she started to feel restless. She was ready for a new adventure, but didn't know where it would lead. This is how she tells the story of what happened next…

"I went to sleep one night in February of 2014 and was awakened at two o'clock in the morning with the mission and vision of Backstory Preaching. I didn't have the name for it yet, but I knew what it was and where it was headed fifteen years into the future.

"This vision funneled all my experience, gifts, education, and deepest passions. The mission was to combine spirituality with preaching, and mentor clergy one-to-one, long-term, like spiritual direction does. Preaching would be the entry point to open their life with God. It would help clergy rely on God as the source of their sermons and fill the void in sermon coaching and feedback that's necessary to gain expertise in any creative endeavor.

"And, it would be done online so it could reach clergy everywhere.

"Finally, after learning to do this myself, clergy who had been through the program could be trained to be mentors. I was up for hours taking notes. Dictation, truly, is what it felt like. It didn't feel like any of it was my idea. Not an ounce of it. As a result, I chose my title to be "Founder and Steward," not "CEO." I was given this vision and believe it is my responsibility to steward it until it's ready to turn over to my successor."

Sometimes, the call really is that clear.

After she received her vision, doors started opening up for Cressman. She met with the Canon to the Ordinary (a priest who assists the bishop), who loved the idea and introduced her to Jackson, the seminary preaching professor she mentioned to me in the email. The two of them launched Backstory Preaching with assistance from a grant in the Diocese of Texas, and they began mentoring clergy in January 2016. As of early 2017, the mentoring program has grown to include a new mentor (me!) and three new mentors-in-training. Cressman supplements the program with master classes, online group sermon preparation, workbook exercises, and a website - backstorypreaching.com.

Her vision didn't end there, though. Soon she began dreaming about how to make sure Backstory Preaching did not remain grant dependent, and that it could be expanded and shared across dioceses and denominations. During this time, she was in deep conversation with Jackson - and with me - and finally, in the spring of 2015, we all met up in Austin, Texas for two days of intensive meeting and brainstorming.

When we were done, Backstory Preaching had become a limited liability company (LLC). It is a church start-up, with a small group of owners and a huge dream to change the world by bringing the vision of effective, Spirit-led preaching to everyone who gets into a pulpit.

Today Backstory Preaching is a full-fledged online and in-person ministry, supporting those who are already ordained across the church, and teaching new preachers in the formation process. In Cressman's words, "we teach preachers how to preach, ground them in spiritual habits, and together, we all become more authentic preachers."

BsP offerings now include online classes, sermon bootcamps and webinars. There is a subscription service that gives access to master classes and other resources, including the e-book, *Craft an Effective Sermon by Friday*. Cressman also wrote *Preaching through Uncertain Times*, to support those in the pulpit bringing Gospel good news in today's politically-charged environment. She offers webinars on this topic as well. She is soon to publish her own book, *The Preacher's Trust: Become a Better Preacher by Integrating Craft with Spirituality*, due to be published in 2017.

Clergy are ordained to live and teach the Christian faith. In this way, Cressman serves her vocation on two levels: she teaches the faith, and she supports those who preach it - and teach it - to others. Through this kind of Free Range Priest ministry, she is able to focus almost exclusively on one aspect of what clergy do. She can then explore this in the deepest ways.

"Preaching is your life. Your life is preaching." This is one of BsP's tag lines, and I love it. It sums up Cressman's ministry, and in a way, it sums up the ministry of all of us who are ordained. Our lives are always preaching. And Cressman's preaching is being heard in pulpits and beyond as a Free Range Priest.

The Evangelist

This time it wasn't an email I received, it was a Facebook message.

"Hi, Cathie. Lisa Cressman said that in addition to interviewing her for The Coffeepot Fellowship Podcast, we should interview you."

At least this time I knew how he found me. The Rev. Jay McNeal is the kind of person you feel like you already know the moment you meet him. Filled with a joyful curiosity that puts others at ease, it seems natural he would regularly interview people as part of his ministry. I was flattered that he wanted to talk with me, and equally curious to know what he was up to. Frankly, I was surprised we hadn't crossed paths before, because what we do is so similar in nature.

I signed up for a time slot to video chat with Jay, and then I got to work listening to the podcast. Luckily, I had a long car trip ahead of me, so I took that time to hear about ten half-hour interviews in a row. I was fascinated.

The Coffeepot Fellowship Podcast, it turns out, is really a collection of conversations with Free Range Priests!

I listened as McNeal drew stories out of people - some ordained, some not - who are sharing the love of God through music, politics, advocacy, and scholarly work. These are ministers who serve in congregations, seminaries, and through websites, podcasts, and books. They lead worship with students, immigrants, people on the margins and those who are not really sure *what* they believe. Most of his guests are Christian, but I also heard from Jews, Muslims, and atheists. I was amazed at the breadth of the experiences and viewpoints of McNeal's guests, and the way he gets them to tell their stories, even those of blunders, setbacks, and failures.

Since it's already right there in the name, everyone interviewed for the podcast is also asked how they take their coffee. I noted that even with this question, diversity is respected. McNeal does not discriminate against those who confess to drinking tea.

After I did my own interview with Jay, I got to know him, and his ministry, a little more. I asked him in an email about Coffeepot Fellowship and its mission. "We can't love one another if we don't know one another," he wrote back. "The podcast lets our listeners get to know others and hopefully models what affirming relationships can be like. We fear what we don't understand. If our show helps people understand then we can replace fear with love and understanding… It's a non-preachy, non-teaching way to change the world by getting in relationship with diverse people."

I also learned that this is not even the main focus of McNeal's ministry. Coffeepot Fellowship (coffeepotfellowship.com) is a way to support United Faith Leaders (unitedfaithleaders.com), a website with a mission to connect faith leaders with the people who are looking for them.

Jay McNeal knows why this ministry is so important.

His own story encompasses four denominations, several forays into theological education (some of them self-led), time in the Army, and moving back and forth across the country. He has endured times of hardship that include bankruptcy, divorce, and near-homelessness. Through all of this, though, he kept hearing God's call to ordained ministry. He completed his seminary education, was ordained in the Baptist Church, and served as a nontraditional minister for online and television congregations. McNeal and his wife are now members of a Unitarian Universalist congregation near their home in Richmond, Virginia. He works in the library of Union Presbyterian Seminary there in addition to his other ministry.

McNeal's life experience has a strong impact on his vision. He explains: "My radical, cynical, wounded, pushed-to-the-fringe self was largely healed and brought to a strong, celebrated "in" center, belonging. It was a good experience to know, but I never forgot or actually left all the people I knew from all my decades with the fringe, marginalized people."

From this, McNeal also learned about the nontraditional ways people are searching for God in their lives, and searching for clergy to lead, guide, and teach them in God's ways. At the same time, there are clergy looking for ways to serve outside the congregation and struggling with how to find them. To address this issue in his own ministry, he told me, he initially created a website and offered pastoral services as a kind of "community chaplain."

Then, he says, "I was shocked at how quickly I was overwhelmed by people searching online for a minister like me. They weren't going to church or denominational websites, they wanted an individual person with a face, someone who they could read about and discern if they would be a good fit."

Soon he expanded his project into United Faith Leaders, a place where faith leaders can create profiles of their ministry, availability, and location, and where people who need their services can easily find them. McNeal's call has become a way for others to answer theirs. He is an evangelist for evangelists.

Imagine my own excitement to discover that this is Free Range Priest ministry by another name! Indeed, as I have continued in conversation with Jay, I am thrilled to discover the ways that our ministries overlap, and how we both understand the stresses of the traditional church model and believe there are ways we can help address them. McNeal shares my own determination to help clergy make the leap across the church threshold into the wider community, but in a way that ultimately supports congregational ministry as well.

"Two thirds of America has no local pastor to call their own," McNeal wrote to me, "but almost every household will have need for a faith leader at some point - for a conversation, funeral, wedding, hospital visit, etc. United Faith Leaders believes in being able to be found so that we can make the love of our traditions manifest in any moment of joy or concern."

What Makes a Free Range Priest

Jabriel Ballentine, Lisa Cressman, and Jay McNeal have distinct ministries, but they also have several things in common.

First, they are all ordained clergy - educated, formed, raised up and guided by the denominational church. Although they serve in Free Range Priest capacities, they serve within the boundaries of the Christian faith and tradition, and they are accountable to it. If people outside of the church are going to trust the ways that Free Range Priest ministry brings the Gospel into their lives, they need to be able to trust the authenticity of the bearer. Being ordained in a faith tradition means, among other things, that clergy bring the trust of the Christian community with them when they meet those beyond the traditional church space.

Free Range Priests also serve doing work that clergy are ordained to do. Just as with congregational clergy, they share good news and equip disciples, live and teach the Christian faith, foster community and care for those in need, stand for justice and question the status quo. They spend time in church, leading worship and preaching, even if most of their ministry takes place outside the walls of it. They may place more emphasis on a certain aspect of this ministry, as Ballentine does on justice and discipleship, Cressman on teaching and preaching, and McNeal on fostering community and sharing good news. But the center of their ministry is not doing *everything*, it is focusing on their own specific gifts and how to share them in the context of the work of clergy.

Each of them also re-thinks the traditional church model in terms of *product* and *process*. Ballentine is a coach and a freelancer. He takes the product - discipleship - and changes the process from something that happens exclusively within a congregation to something that can happen anywhere, in any aspect of our lives. Through his relationship coaching, he helps people see how following Jesus impacts every choice they make in their lives. Through his podcast, he challenges listeners to examine their own lives and attitudes in the light of the self-giving love of Jesus. On his website, he writes, speaks, and teaches in ways that reach anyone who finds themselves there, whether they are church members or not. In all of this, he finds new venues for the traditional work of a pastor in a congregation.

Cressman is a teacher and a spiritual start-up. She is taking the craft of preaching, a product very basic to what clergy do, and changing the process of how they learn it. Most clergy get only a couple of courses on preaching in the midst of all their other education, then they are sent out into the world to do it on a regular basis. Cressman says it is like taking a series of introductory violin lessons, and then being sent on a concert tour - where you will write the music and perform it! Add to this the ways that seminary education is changing, and it is easy to see how many preachers feel inadequately prepared for this sacred role. Cressman re-imagines the process in terms of *backstory* - how the preacher's own spiritual life is developing, and also *preaching* - what makes an effective sermon and how to offer one. She uses non-traditional methods of delivery, like online courses and meetings, but the real difference in process is about how preachers are formed and supported in their task.

McNeal is re-thinking the whole structure. If Free Range Priests are called to re-claim officiating at weddings and funerals from the secular world, they need a place to find those looking for actual clergy who are ready and willing to do so. If they are looking to freelance in any capacity, they need a way to let others know what they do. If they are looking for a community of like-minded clergy for support and sharing experiences, they need to feel like they are not alone. McNeal takes administration -

which is a product we don't often think of in terms of ministry, although it is very necessary - and changes the process so that it becomes a much more flexible platform for Free Range Priests to be connected to the people who need their work. This is not the authority structure. Clergy are still ordained and overseen by their denominations. It is the process by which ordained clergy and those whom they serve can be matched. This process is innovative in that it can reach across denominations with ease, while still respecting the differences of each.

Digital Free Range Priest

Another way these three Free Range Priests are alike is they do a great deal of work online. Digital ministry is non-negotiable in the church today, and it goes far beyond each church having a website and a Facebook page. Clergy, no matter where or how they serve, need to be social media savvy. There is lots of advice about this along the lines of how to protect one's boundaries and privacy when engaging others online, and this is prudent. But it doesn't go far enough.

We live in an era when an online presence is assumed, and if someone does not have one, we might get a little suspicious of them. Professional life of any kind virtually requires (pun intended) that others are able to get a sense of us from Google. Much more importantly, sharing the Gospel and creating community are part of the job description of all Christians, and certainly all clergy. Social media is designed to help us connect to lots of other people and promote things about who we are and what we believe. It is practically an evangelism toolkit. Using it is incredibly important.

Not everyone is comfortable with this idea. Mainline denominational Christians tend to be a pretty traditional bunch, and are older than the general population. This is also true for clergy. Sometimes social media is hard to figure out, sometimes it is intimidating, there are well-founded concerns about privacy and vulnerability when using it. It is also well-known that not everyone practices courtesy and kindness in the digital world, especially when discussing politics and religion. All of these are understandable reasons to give careful consideration when assessing our online presence. But they are not sufficient reasons to decline it.

Besides evangelism, social media gives us a chance to know the people we serve in ways that we probably never would in the congregation, or wherever else we might meet them. When I was a parish priest, I thought I knew my members pretty well, and they told me when they were ill or suffering or struggling, or when someone they loved was in distress. But once I was on Facebook, I found out so much more. I knew what their everyday lives were like, their joys and challenges and the funny thing they saw at the grocery store. I knew if their dog was sick or their kid got an A on a test or made the basketball team (or did not). There were so many more ways I could enter their lives and point to where God was there, too.

And social media has done more for my prayer life than anything I have learned since seminary.

Every day I see prayer requests from people I know and people I don't, and I stop and pray right then. I also ask for prayer in my own life as I go through my digital day. And once a year, on All Saint's Day, I pray for every single one of my Facebook friends - and I have over 1,500 of them! It takes hours, but it is well worth it. Family, friends, colleagues, people I know from church and random strangers get a moment to be lifted up. I know, too, that plenty of my Facebook friends also practice this form of prayer, so I feel confident that I am prayed for every day. There is a lot of talk among church people around whether or not online relationships and community are "real." I know that my prayers - and others' - are definitely real, and that makes me pretty confident that makes for real connection. This alone is reason for clergy - for all Christians - to be on social media for the sake of practicing our faith.

Of course it goes beyond this, too. Ballentine, Cressman and McNeal each have websites and Facebook pages for their respective ministries. They blog, send out newsletters, post videos, host webinars, teach classes, sell books, and produce podcasts, all online. It is safe to say that their ministries would not exist if it were not for the proliferation of ways we can now interact in the virtual world. Neither would mine.

It is harder and harder to distinguish between "real" life and the one we enter into through technology. This is not all good news, which is true today in the same way that it was true when the printing press was invented, or the first book was bound. There are things that are lost - how we used to memorize stories and hand them down, the people we entrusted with bodies of knowledge and tools of power. As these things change in today's world, there are dangers for sure. Yet I don't think it is an exaggeration to say the church could not survive if it did not exist online. Because that's where the people are, that's where they are relating, sharing themselves, conducting business, creating art, and looking for God.

"People all over the world were getting online at every minute of every day seeking a personal faith leader," Jay McNeal reminds us.

"All while faith leaders are burning out in their shrinking churches. The technology should already exist to solve this problem but it doesn't. Faith leaders should already all be in one database, searchable by zip code and other filters, but they don't. The world should be able to see faith leaders working together side by side, but they don't. We can fix this."

McNeal's ministry is one example of how important online presence is, in every facet of who we are as clergy and what we do as the church. In the same way, Cressman's ability to teach preaching in Minnesota from her home in Texas, while sharing the duties with me in North Carolina, is bringing resources and support to those who might not get them if they had to rely on what is available within 50 miles of their rural home. And Ballentine's voice of hope in the midst of hard times is invaluable in a culture that has generally turned away from God just when we need good news the most.

Ironically, online ministry might be the very tool we need the most to bring people back into the traditional church. One gift we have, those of us who worship in stone buildings with worn books and beautiful windows and vintage organs, is an actual sacred space. A real, physical place where you can feel the prayers seeping from the stones, where you can sing right next to other people, shake their hands and say "good morning," and gather around an altar to receive real bread and real wine. And feel God's real presence. This is an enormous gift to the world, even the world that no longer believes. We believe for them. These places exist for us all.

Yet since there are fewer and fewer of us there, there are more and more of us who don't know about it. Who have never experienced this. Being online, talking about our faith and our church on social media, explaining and sharing our ministry through blogs and podcasts, this is how we reach people. Praying for and with others virtually can be a step to doing so in person. Those who have never been to church, or never been to our church, might be moved to do so if they know us online. The era of strangers just walking into our buildings is pretty much over. But if we meet them in the digital world, we have a chance to welcome them in real life.

The Free Range Priest challenge

This straddling of worlds - ancient faith practices, traditional church models, and new online ministry, is both the beauty and the puzzle for Free Range Priests. There is so much work to do, in so many ways, and we are limited only by our call from God and our vision for where that can take us.

There are a few challenges, too. One is finding the balance between being bearers of institutional religion while not being bound to the institution in certain ways. How 'free' are we as Free Range Priests? We want to find innovative ways to share the Gospel, but also keep the authority that has been bestowed on us to do this.

McNeal explains how he understands it: "I may be relatively Free Range because there is some distance between me and any human being looking closely over my shoulder, scrutinizing every word choice and decision. I am free not to follow God or what God is calling me to do. But in my freedom I feel quite entirely bound to give my heart, soul and gifts back to God and humanity."

In some ways, this is a constant discernment of our call to ordination. When we serve in a congregation, the clarity of what we do there is itself a balance for our vocation. Knowing what work is expected of us helps us know who we are as clergy, the importance of what we do in terms of how it affects the lives of others. When we are separated from this, we need to assert our understanding of ourselves as ordained people in a way that is assumed when we serve traditionally. The 'free range' part of the call might be clear, but the 'priest' part may need some explanation, for others and for ourselves.

This brings light to another challenge - how we stay connected in community. Cressman says she is still "living into" the idea of being a Free Range Priest. "The term raises images of roaming and rootlessness," she says, the opposite of what being ordained is about, which is holding us together in tradition and faith. "Is it possible to be both?" she wonders. "To offer ministry where the Spirit's wind moves us, yet still feel grounded as an integral part of a wider community of priests?"

I feel certain it is possible, but this is all part of the growing and changing church. I am reminded again of how congregations call themselves *family*. There is a comfort and security to this, and at the same time, it is very enclosed. If no one ever leaves a family, even for a time, there will be no new members brought in, no new experiences or viewpoints to share. Families who are completely insular - whether church families or biological ones - will eventually die off. There needs to be new life brought in, and to do that, there needs to be space for members to venture off, and to come home.

This is true for actual families, for church families, and for the wider church. New ways to explore our ministry as clergy means fresh expressions of faith for all. If we never go out from the traditional model, we risk our ministry dying altogether. But we need to come home, too. We can't ignore the ways we are connected to the institutional church, and how necessary this is for our vocation, our lives, and the faith itself. Finding this balance will always be before us as Free Range Priests.

Another balance is the financial one. Clergy who work in traditional ways worry about whether the congregation can continue to afford their salary, or whether they will be able to find another full-time position. Free Range Priests worry about whether we will find enough work to cover our bills. Spiritual start-ups are exciting, but unlike, say, tech start-ups, there are not usually investors lining up to help us secure capital. Free Range Priest ministry offers possibilities of new ways and places to get paid for our work. It does not, however, offer certainty.

All three of the Free Range Priests I know are still working on that balance. Cressman has a firm business plan and excellent guidance, and still she needs to project her profits into the future. Backstory Preaching is successful, spiritually and financially, but it is also still getting off the ground.

Ballentine also sees this kind of ministry as a process in every way, including financially. When asked how he would advise others considering Free Range Priest ministry, he says he would want them "to be sure they have a way to sustain themselves and their family, and the requisite skill to execute that sustainability plan." McNeal concurs, and lists as one of his ministry challenges: "providing for my family and paying my student loans."

This is why I believe being a Free Range Priest can be a hybrid of serving inside and outside of a congregation. New ministry is exciting, but it is a bit of a leap in terms of both accountability and financial solvency. Traditional congregational ministry is more proscribed, but comes with the tension of whether and how it can be sustained.

There is a middle way in this: clergy serving Free Range for some hours within the congregation and some outside of it, at the same time. This may grant both the flexibility and the grounding necessary for congregations - especially small ones - to keep up their own ministry, and for clergy to thrive in theirs. This will take a willingness on the part of clergy, congregations, and larger denominational structures to recognize the importance of both new and traditional ministry, and how it all works together.

How we all benefit from this is the opening of possibility. One of the reasons money is so hard to talk about in church is that we don't know what to do about the dilemma of not having enough to sustain clergy salary and building maintenance with just congregational giving to support it. Not having any viable options besides closing churches or clergy not getting paid can lead us to places where fear constricts us. When there are other options for ministry that is affordable for both, we all benefit from the *free* part of Free Range Priest ministry: freedom to focus on sharing our faith.

McNeal describes his ministry like this: "United Faith Leaders recognizes that feuding, selfish, scared faith leaders are destructive and repel people. Clinging to money, buildings, and people makes for something unlike the kingdom of heaven on earth. On the contrary, secure, open, generous, cooperative faith leaders make for peace and love. It may not save any particular building or job position but it does deliver freedom to everyone to choose and discern who, who's and how they will walk their life's path.

This aligns very closely with the mission of Free Range Priest ministry. When clergy have options of ways to serve their vocation, they are renewed in it. And they bring this sense of renewal to the work they do with congregations as well as the work they do outside of them. This is incredibly beneficial to clergy, and to those they are able to reach with the Gospel doing non-traditional ministry. It is also beneficial to congregations and their mission.

7. Free Range Priest and the Congregation

Part of the good news of thinking creatively about ministry is the new opportunities for clergy. Free Range Priests are bringing the Gospel to the world in every way we can think of, every day. While much ministry is still in its start-up phase, there is lots of hope and optimism among those I have spoken with.

This is not to say that traditional congregational ministry is devoid of innovation or life. In fact, part of the overall good news of re-imagining how clergy serve is that we can find ways to serve both congregations and the wider mission field. This is good news for clergy, as it gives us connection stability, both spiritually and financially.

It's good news for congregations, too.

It is especially good news for smaller churches, those often caught in the triangle of trying to sustain their mission and ministry while also affording a clergy salary and the upkeep of a building. Since this is a tension felt by at least half of the congregations in the Episcopal Church, and many more in other denominations, it's good news worth considering from the perspective of the traditional church model. How can a mainline Christian church benefit from working with a Free Range Priest?

St. Paul's Episcopal Church in Salisbury, North Carolina, is a good example of how this question might be answered, and a place I know well. It is a pretty brick church situated on a modest corner of a historic mill town about 45 miles east of Charlotte with a population of about 30,000. They have a unique history, and they share a story with thousands of other places like them - small congregations in places that were once thriving and now a little sleepier. In a faith tradition that was once the center of life for the whole community, and now struggles to appeal to those of different generations and life choices.

The church was founded in 1887 in the Chestnut Hill section of Salisbury by the Rev. Francis Johnstone Murdoch, a charismatic and powerful preacher who was instrumental in developing both the economic and religious life of the city. Murdoch helped establish the first textile mills (and was a stockholder in them) to help the poor of Salisbury improve their lot in life. He also served as a priest at the neighboring (and much larger) St. Luke's Episcopal Church downtown, and spearheaded the establishment of St. Paul's and 11 other missions in the area.

At a certain point during Murdoch's expansive and sometimes controversial ministry, the vestry (governing board) of St. Paul's expressed concern that their priest was also a businessman in town, perhaps creating a conflict of interest. Murdoch reportedly heard their concerns, and then responded: "Gentlemen, if I end my business interests in this town, you'll all go poor, and if I resign as rector of this parish you'll all go to hell. Therefore I choose neither - next order of business[49]."

This quote, to me, captures the spirit of St. Paul's - resolutely faithful and practical in their ministry, full of can-do spirit and determination, sprinkled with plain-spoken opinions and good humor. St. Paul's is like many small congregations across the Episcopal Church - it has known boom and bust, it has a long and storied past and it has often struggled for its very survival. Today, its future is as uncertain as it ever has been.

Which is not to say that there is no hope, because this congregation has seen lean times followed by better ones before. According to the wonderful church history written in 1987 as a centennial anniversary gift by Vicar Allen Webster Joslin, St. Paul's struggled after Murdoch's death in 1909, and well into the 1920s. At that time they kept employing supply priests, as they were unable to find a vicar (priest of a mission church) of their own[50].

Between the 1920s and 50s, they had their own priests, along with stability and modest growth in buildings and population. This time corresponded with the height of church attendance in the United States. But the 1970s brought lean times - for St. Paul's and for the mainline church in general - and the historic church on Chestnut Hill almost closed.

There were thoughts of merging it with St. Luke's, or making it a mission of the larger church, which would have meant letting St. Paul's keep its identity and be served by St. Luke's clergy, but would have put the church at risk of eventually being subsumed altogether. Several dramatic meetings with the bishop were held. At the 11th hour, a new vicar for St. Paul's was found and they held on to their own mission once again[51].

Since that time, there have perhaps been fewer cliffhangers in the life of this congregation, but more steady decline, which matches the decline of the larger denomination and mainline Christianity itself. Through it all, St. Paul's has maintained its worship, faithful commitment to its members and community, and its own special spirit.

In 1961, the Rev. H. Hunt Comer wrote in his own historical sketch (quoted in the one done by Joslin) that while St. Paul's "was never a large church, it has always been noted for its friendly and informal atmosphere combined with devotional richness and abiding faith in the Church heritage of two thousand years characteristic of the Episcopal Church. Strangers who frequently worship here have commented on the beautiful services and the sacredness of the atmosphere of St. Paul's[52]."

This was my impression the first time I served there, on Easter Sunday 2016.

Their last vicar, the Rev. Richard (Rick) Williams, a retired Naval chaplain, had been with them from 2012 until his retirement at the end of 2015, and during that time he had led something of a revival at St. Paul's. Using an energy that matched the congregation's, they worked together with neighboring churches and community organizations to pool resources and offer services to the poor and struggling in the area. Their outreach ministry and involvement with their neighbors belied the small number of parishioners in the pews.

All this work has not changed the dynamics of the failing system that congregations and clergy are serving in. After Williams' retirement, St. Paul's finds itself in the same place, demographically and financially, as it did in 1910 and 1975. Only this time, the world and the church have changed so much that finding a new clergyperson is far from certain.

St. Paul's has about 60 members on the books (and about half that on any given Sunday), who solely support the ministry and facilities. They have no endowment to dip into when things fall short. Lay people, by necessity, do pretty much all the work of the congregation: scheduling clergy for Sunday morning, and saying lay-led Morning Prayer if they can't get a priest; teaching Sunday school and other Christian formation; planning for the church year, liturgically and musically; all outreach and pastoral care; building maintenance and administration; dealing with any conflicts or problems that arise.

Because of their history, the lay leaders at St. Paul's are used to doing all the work it takes to run a church. Sometimes they have clergy to do this work with them, and sometimes they don't, so they have to be prepared to be their own spiritual and community leaders. And they are.

Part of that leadership is discerning where St. Paul's will go next.

They are probably unable to afford a new part-time vicar at this point. Rick Williams, like many retired clergy working part-time in small congregations, put in many more hours than he was paid for. Today's clergy, many of whom are not yet of retirement age, or not receiving a pension, cannot afford to do this. So there are fewer clergy choices for them, and the ones they have will need a salary that St. Paul's may not be able to afford. They hope to grow their membership, but in a small town and a generally declining denomination, it does not seem realistic or likely that they will be able to significantly increase it. This is a time of hope but maybe not as much optimism.

Some may hear this story and wonder if it is just time for this particular church to close. St. Luke's, the "big church" in Salisbury, is just a mile away, and the members of St. Paul's could attend there. If St. Paul's does not have the resources or the membership to sustain itself, why should it be kept open for the small number of people who are still there? This is a question that is being asked all across the church today.

One answer certainly is to let St. Paul's close and figure that is just the way things go - congregations have life cycles just like people do. We all die someday. But I am convinced it is not the only answer.

Almost 1,000 small congregations in the Episcopal Church alone are in the same place, too small to afford even a very part-time priest. If we say goodbye to St. Paul's, we are saying goodbye to about 20 percent of our congregations across the church, some in locations where there is not another Episcopal presence - maybe not another church at all - for many miles. And even if they were all in very populated places, each congregation has its own history, character, and mission. Just like with people, we all die - and it is a loss every time. No one wants to hasten the demise of a place with so much love and faith.

I don't think we have to.

Small congregations have some big gifts, and one of them is the possibility, and in some cases the necessity, to do things a little differently in order to survive and thrive in today's church. No one really likes to change. We would all like to see the church grow without having to do much of anything differently than we have before. It's easy, when we have more resources, to keep pushing off the tightening budget or slipping attendance numbers to next year, making do with what we have now, because we can. For now.

But when we have few enough members that every Sunday and every budget decision clearly count in terms of our short-term and long-term survival as a community, making changes is no longer really optional. This can be hard, but it can also open doors of possibility. There are some changes that will not disrupt the basic model of church, just make it more affordable, and potentially better for clergy and congregations.

Churches like St. Paul's are a perfect match for a Free Range Priest. Small congregations need enough of a clergyperson's time to support ministry but not so much that it actually becomes burdensome. Free Range Priests need a place - often more than one - to connect their ministry with the church and the world. Together they can each support each other, and not just financially. Re-thinking how clergy might serve with congregations can have benefits in terms of how congregations thrive spiritually, too.

Free Range Priests support lay ministry

Changing the way clergy are paid, and for what, also changes the relationship dynamics between them and the congregations they serve. No longer are clergy there for *everything*, but for the time and the tasks that they set together with the lay leadership of the church. Clergy are there on particular Sundays or days of the week, for instance, but not all of them. Or they contract for monthly pastoral care or teaching hours and serve them as they are able. When they are not with the congregation, they may be serving in another one, or online, or in another ministry capacity. They do not become the priest that belongs to the congregation and is always there.

This changes the traditional way clergy and congregation relate.

Years ago, I was working with a different small congregation (also called St. Paul's, coincidentally), they were discerning whether they had the resources and the inclination to move from regular supply clergy on Sundays to a new part-time vicar of their own. It was a very honest discussion, and although they had the money for a part-time salary, they were torn about whether they really wanted a new priest who spent significant time with them. Intrigued, I asked why they might not want a new vicar. One parishioner put it like this:

"When we don't have our own priest, a small group of us make all the decisions and do all the work ourselves, and we get tired. We know we need help. Then we get a new priest, and we hand all that work over to them, and we are relieved. At first it is great, and more people start coming to church. But then the priest is doing everything, and making every decision. And some people don't like that, or they don't like the decisions the priest is making. And so they leave. And then, eventually, the priest leaves. And then a small group of us is doing all the work and making all the decisions again..."

This was a lightbulb moment in my ministry. Clergy doing *everything* in a congregation are not just burning ourselves out, and potentially losing sight of the work we are called to do. We are also disrupting, and maybe even interfering with, the lay leadership in small congregations. This happens in ways we often don't even see, and goes back to whether clergy work *with* a congregation or *for* a congregation. Clergy are the natural leaders when we serve in the traditional model. But do we have the final say in all decisions?

This is a tricky place to negotiate, and we sometimes defer it. This means, as this wise parishioner explained, that we might be unintentionally making decisions that are better taken on by lay leadership. Or we may be doing work that is really lay ministry. There are lots of ways we try to foster ministry, but end up doing most of it ourselves. Or we set the vision and try to get everyone on board, instead of waiting with them for the vision to appear. Sometimes it is simply a matter of feeling like certain things just won't get done without us.

I remember a time I was visiting with a fellow priest - just catching up, getting some lunch. As I drove into the parking lot of his church to meet him, I saw him out in the yard, mowing the lawn. This was not a young man - at this point he was easily in his late 70s. And it was a hot day.

After he cooled off and cleaned up and we were on our way, I questioned him a little, both for doing yard work in the middle of a summer day at his age, and also for doing yard work at all as the clergyperson of a church. He was not amused, and did not take kindly to either my ageism or my presumption about his ministry.

"There are only about 50 people total in this congregation," he said to me with exasperation. "All of them are at least as old as me, and most of them are women. We can't afford to pay someone to mow the lawn. Who else is going to do it? I can and I do pray while I take care of the yard. I think about my sermon. I listen for God's voice. But this is my congregation and I love and serve them, so I am going to mow the lawn when it needs it."

Point taken. I completely understood, then and now, how much he loved the church he served and saw it as his duty to care for them in many ways. I do not mean to imply that his ministry with them wasn't important, or that mowing the lawn is "lay ministry." It is just that when a clergyperson is with a congregation all the time, they can tend to see all aspects of its life as their mission field. Sometimes this is enormously helpful.

Sometimes it gets in the way of lay leaders discerning what is best for the church. In this case, it may have been time to hire someone to mow the lawn. It may have even been time to sell some of the land the church owned, or offer it for a dog park or a community garden. By continuing to just do it himself, my faithful friend may have been inadvertently cutting off other options for this community.

A Free Range Priest has a different perspective because of the way we serve. We are necessarily limited in our tasks in one place, so even if we have the inclination, we do not have the ability do *everything* in a congregation. Because of this we have to choose more carefully what we do, and also what we do *not* do.

Free Range Priests lead worship, preach and administer the sacraments. We teach the faith and form disciples. We gather community and care for those in need. And we do so in a way that leaves a lot of space for lay ministers to do their own work in the areas. Lay people most certainly have worship roles, and also those in teaching, discipleship, prayer, music, outreach and many others. They also usually have a long history of doing ministry in this particular place. And though they may need clergy for guidance and resources, they also have their own body of knowledge and experience to draw from in their spiritual leadership. The role of the clergyperson is to support, guide, and care for lay leaders, not to do their work for them.

Serving only certain hours or days with a congregation has a built-in boundary on how involved we can be in its everyday life. This in turn can be a way to ensure that clergy do not become *overly* involved in the mission of the church, leaving space for the true development of lay leadership. This is especially important when congregations are discerning how they will fulfill their mission, which decisions they will make about their future and where God is calling them. These can be large things like whether to start a new ministry or even relocate, or smaller ones like which hymnal to use or whether or not to have an egg hunt on Easter. Lay leaders often defer to clergy on decisions, no matter the size, and clergy must take care to support lay leaders' vision instead. The Free Range Priest has this advantage because we know we are not there to do *everything*.

All believers have the same mission and the same call to be followers of Jesus, whether we are ordained or not. When we are ordained, we are instilled with knowledge, formation and authority to carry the tradition in a primary way, as a living source of the tradition itself. We are a special resource for other believers, but we don't take away the responsibility each disciple has to grow and share their faith. We are in a sense like a doctor - each person's health is their own, and they make choices about it every day. And when they need assistance managing their health, they seek out someone trained more fully in the area to give advice and recommendations, which they then choose to abide by or not.

As a clergyperson, I am a doctor of the soul. I refer people to the medicine of Scripture and sacrament, tradition and prayer, to help them make choices and decisions that lead them on the path of faith and that help them become more spiritually healthy. I am not in any way more faithful or more knowledgeable than they are. I am a resource, a coach, a vessel of what they need to be the best disciples they can be. Being a Free Range Priest helps me keep perspective on this, and in this way helps support lay leadership.

Free Range Priests support congregations in conflict

The tensions felt by many traditional churches have already been described in this book. These tensions - over shrinking budgets and numbers, and rising needs, can sometimes play out within a congregation. Add to this the long-term dynamics of any group of people over time, and soon enough, most congregations have to deal with conflict.

Clergy are not generally thrilled about conflict in the congregation, and often feel undertrained to deal with it. When I was serving the Diocese of North Carolina as a Canon, I facilitated a program called *Fresh Start*, designed to support clergy in new positions. We had many modules for topics, too many to cover in the time allotted. So I would ask the program participants which topics were most interesting to them. Conflict was always one of them. In fact, we had three conflict modules, and we used all three. Clergy simply felt ill-prepared for some of the dynamics they encountered, and they feared being caught up in them, too. Some of them were under attack themselves, and not sure how to respond.

We know, as Christians, that we have a natural antidote to unhealthy conflict: we follow Jesus. Commitment to the Gospel can make church a place of mediation and peaceful resolution. Sin, forgiveness, reconciliation and redemption are the very cornerstones of what we believe and practice in our lives.

This does not mean facing conflict is easy. It takes faith, courage, vulnerability and love. It is a learned practice that needs to be sustained within a community for it to productive. And in my experience, it takes a little distance, too. This is one reason we have programs like *Fresh Start*: support and reflection for those who need perspective on issues.

One challenge for clergy is how to address congregational conflict without being caught up in it ourselves, and without becoming the focal point of it. It is tricky to maintain enough distance from its source of that we can serve as guides in faithful resolution and not get embroiled. Clergy can take sides in disagreements, whether intentionally or not, thus putting ourselves in the situation of winning or losing an issue. Unfortunately, there are even times when clergy are a source of conflict, either deepening divides between others or causing discord with our actions (or inactions). This is a particularly difficult situation and often needs outside help and support to work through. Conflict is also a reason clergy leave a position, especially when it is constant or unresolved.

Sometimes congregations leave because of conflict, too, or individual members do. When this happens, relationships are cut off rather than resolved, and so the wounds remain and never heal. There is no reconciliation, no real peace. The community is not only fractured, but it is vulnerable to repeating the same dynamic again with a different group of people, because whatever is conflicted has not been resolved. All these situations are not just emotionally damaging, they are a missed opportunity for spiritual growth, individually and as a community.

All clergy, regardless of how we serve, deal with conflict eventually. Free Range Priests are not necessarily any better trained or constitutionally equipped to deal with it than those who serve in traditional ways. But the non-traditional relationship that a Free Range Priest has with a congregation can be helpful.

Serving set hours and days creates some distance between clergy and congregation, both literally and in terms of dynamics between them. So when a conflict arises, Free Range Priests can approach it more like a spiritual consultant than someone who has ultimate say in the matter. This can give us a more neutral stance, from which we can offer wisdom, prayer, and guidance without trying to solve the issue.

This distance also gives us the potential to speak more freely in the community, especially if there is open conflict or bad behavior. Underneath some differences there is fear of how someone will react if they are confronted over an attitude or decision. Sometimes salaried clergy can even fear for their jobs because if a member of a church were to leave, especially one who happened to give a lot of money to the church, it could have an effect on the budget. Whether consciously or not, this can cause clergy to hold their tongue. A Free Range Priest is not dependent on one congregation for their livelihood and thus does not have this concern.

And frankly, if a situation is hostile, a Free Range Priest does not have to live with it all the time. Being able to come and go, and having other places to serve in ministry, helps breathe fresh air into a conflict that may feel consuming. This is helpful for the clergyperson to keep a calm perspective, and they can then share this with the congregation.

All of these advantages have to do with *how* the Free Range Priest serves in a congregation, not whether they are particularly skilled at conflict resolution or particular thick-skinned when dealing with disagreements. Free Range Priests are still *priests*, and like our salaried counterparts face the same challenges. It is the way we serve that can give us new ways to approach ministry and support congregations. It is the same *product*, just a different *process*.

Free Range Priests support sustainability

There is no question that the biggest benefit for small congregations working with Free Range Priests is financial. If churches pay contractually for clergy work, then they can can figure out how much ordained ministry they need and pay for only that. For some congregations, this is the difference between staying open or not.

Traditionally, congregations pay for full-time, half-time or quarter-time salaried ministry. The average full-time compensation (salary and benefits) in the Episcopal Church is $60,000 for congregations of 75 members or fewer[53]. So even quarter-time ministry would cost $15,000 a year. Plenty of congregations struggle to pay this, and even if they do, they struggle to pay for anything else beyond it.

Options are usually limited in this situation. Congregations can spend money on clergy salary until it runs out and they close. They can either merge with another congregation or share a clergy salary with one or more other churches. They can call supply clergy on Sunday only, or they can find clergy who will serve with them for free. All of these options are viable for a time, and all of them have drawbacks.

Congregations using most of their money to pay for clergy ministry usually end up with clergy who are working way more than they should for very little pay. Clergy know when congregations are spending most of their money on ordained ministry, so out of love they usually try and do *everything* in return. Unfortunately, this leads to burnout, tension, and other dynamic difficulties between them. Ultimately, it also leaves the congregation without resources. Sharing clergy between churches is difficult for the similar reasons. Clergy can feel like they have multiple full-time jobs for part-time pay, and congregations feel like they pay too much and see too little of their clergy. Churches become like strange siblings, vying over who gets their joint clergyperson for what occasion, especially around holidays.

Merging with other congregations often brings tension over buildings and whether they will have to be sold, and members who resist combining communities. There is an idea that if one church closes, its members will go to another nearby, but this isn't always true. When we consider how deeply congregations feel like *family*, it is not so surprising that when they close, members often stop going to church at all.

Long-term Sunday supply is a viable solution for worship and sacraments, but leaves congregations without any Christian formation, pastoral care, or other ordained ministry. Finding clergy who serve for free is a benefit for individual congregations, but harmful to the whole church in the long run (more on this in Chapter 8).

Free Range Priest ministry looks at all the traditional options and aims to provide as many of the benefits as possible with as few of the drawbacks. The most important benefit is that congregations themselves do not have to change. They get to keep their building, their worship, their leaders, and their ways of doing things. They do not have to give up their own ministry or activities and they do not have to share their clergy.

They are not asked to pay more than they can afford in order to have worship, pastoral care, hospital visits and funerals. A congregation with at least 10 members should be able to stay open indefinitely if they want to.

A Free Range Priest will work with the congregation for the hours they can afford. One drawback is they may not be with them every Sunday. One benefit is they can be available for ministry that occurs during the rest of the week. In this way, Free Range Priest ministry is like extended supply.

A Free Range Priest does not get paid a salary, but does get paid for the work they do. This means they are affordable for small congregations, and also able to sustain themselves in ministry, which in turn supports all congregations in the long run. If ministry is free, then not only is it de-valued generally, it eventually leads to clergy being unable to sustain themselves at all.

Free Range Priest is not the answer to all the issues currently facing the institutional church. It is another option, though, for some of the tensions felt by congregations and clergy in their ministry right now. And in these ways it can be a particularly supportive option for small congregations.

Free Range Priests support emerging congregations

It can also be very helpful when congregations are new.

Being able to afford clergy is crucial when worshiping communities are just starting out. The current church planting model of the Episcopal Church, like other mainline denominations, tends to follow along with the traditional building/clergy/congregation model that established congregations usually follow.

Because they are new, and often small, emerging congregations generally get some kind of help affording this. Sometimes they meet in an unusual space, like a restaurant or a school gym or a synagogue (not used on Sunday), so that they can be spared the full cost of space. Sometimes they "inherit" a congregation, a group of members from another church who intentionally leave to start a new mission. And sometimes the salary of their clergyperson is paid through a grant, or supported through the budget of other established churches. These are ways, over time, that the larger denominations have tried to foster the birth and growth of new congregations.

In doing my research for this book, I was curious to know how it was working - how many new congregations across the Episcopal Church are being formed and how they are doing. When I delved into it, I could hardly find any information at all. Then I finally did find something.

According to the Episcopal Church's research, as of 2014 only 3 percent of all congregations were formed in the last 20 years[54]. Between 1994 and 2014, only 200 congregations were started, out of 6,553[55] total in the church.

I was prepared to write about Free Range Priests as those who can help make the church planting model work a little better. The same benefits to small established congregations - room for more lay leadership, guidance in conflict, affordable ministry - would be the same for new ones. An emerging congregation would not have to feel burdened by paying a full or part-time clergy salary, or worrying about how they might do so once the grant or other support ended.

This is true but academic in light of the fact that we are barely starting any new congregations at all. This is rather dire news in a world so hungry for the Gospel, and in a church so rapidly losing members. On the other hand, as so many leave church, and those who are left face increasing challenges to keep their doors open, it should not seem terribly surprising that there is not a lot of energy or resources left over to start new communities.

This makes Free Range Priest ministry even more important and valuable. Right now, starting a new congregation takes months, if not years of planning. One of the main pieces of the puzzle is how to find a clergyperson willing to do the worship, sacramental and formation work necessary to start a church, for the salary available. It is usually a great deal of work for a moderate amount of pay, and it is not guaranteed far into the future.

Church-planting is hard work, especially in a traditional model that is not working as well as it used to. Even clergy who are very mission-minded, and excited to start new churches, are still reluctant to step out into something that feels so financially shaky and administratively burdensome.

A Free Range Priest does not have the same risk factor, and may not have the same organizational factor, either. If a worshiping community only has to pay us for the time they need our ministry, then the financial burden is not as large. There may be more lay ministry involved in a church plant, it may take a little longer to get going. A Free Range Priest may be able to meet with a new congregation only twice a month, but that might be all they need at first.

If they also find a place to meet that is free or very affordable, then they can keep their ministry in line with their growth. In this way, a very small and casual congregation can form, maybe ten or 12 people meeting in a space that is free or nearly so. For $50 a person, they can afford ordained ministry, who can lead worship, teach about the faith, and coach them in their discipleship. This group is free to meet together as long as they like - maybe they grow and become a more established congregation, maybe they all eventually move to other congregations already in existence, maybe the drift off and re-form into other worshiping communities.

No matter what happens, the emerging congregation has the opportunity to have clergy when they need them, but they are not forced to worry about supporting them into an uncertain future. And the Free Range Priest, with other ministry happening in other areas, is not fully dependent on this one congregation, and so can encourage them to move in whatever direction God is calling them. This model is much more lay ministry dependent, and it is much more agile. Many new congregations can form this way, with some existing a short while and some lasting longer, with much more structural ease than having to plan long term for a building and a clergy salary, and much more freedom to spend their time and energy on mission and ministry.

Because this is not happening anywhere I know of at the moment, I can only offer this as a vision. But we live in times that call for vision, especially within the church. Free Range Priest ministry allows for the possibility of thinking in this direction for those hoping to start new congregations. I am sure this is just one of many other directions, as well.

Free Range Priests support larger congregations, too

Whether they have existed for over 125 years like St. Paul's in Salisbury, NC, or they have not yet begun to exist at all, groups of lay people who worship God together have the chance to re-think their ministry with the Free Range Priest model. It is a small but significant change that offers new ways to consider the relationship between clergy and congregation.

Not all traditional congregations are like St. Paul's, of course. There are churches like St. Mark's in Huntersville, bigger and thriving. There are very large churches with lots of resources and staff. There are certainly churches in the traditional model that are growing, changing, looking forward and easily affording full-time or part-time clergy ministry. These churches, too, could see benefit from Free Range Priest ministry. Sometimes a clergyperson is on sabbatical, or takes a medical leave, and a congregation needs a coverage for a short period of time. Maybe there is a particular season when the priest is starting a new ministry and would like someone else to preach for a few weeks in a row. Or there have been several deaths in a parish at once and they need help with funerals. Sometimes a congregation can afford one full-time clergy salary, but not two, and there really is more work than one ordained person can handle. They might need another one to help out a few hours a week, or a couple Sundays a month.

There are many ways that a Free Range Priest can supplement the salaried ministry that is already happening in congregations. Beyond this, when small congregations are thriving, it supports the whole church. This has benefits for larger congregations, too. We all share the same mission field, and when ministry is sustained in rural areas or with smaller groups, it builds up all those who are growing in discipleship.

This does require a change in concept about how clergy serve, though. A change that is small but has larger implications for the institutional church. Clergy are not usually seen as freelancers. This may seem odd in the secular world, but it is strange for the church, too. Mainline Christian denominations are set up to support clergy in salaried positions in congregations (or other institutional settings).

There is generally no administrative mechanism, or basic mindset, to think about how or where one might fit clergy into short-term roles or contract work.

Ordained ministers serve in interim capacities between times when congregations have more permanent clergy, but these are usually full-time jobs that are temporary but relatively long term - a year or more. If a larger congregation wanted to hire a clergyperson to teach a class on Wednesday nights for three months, it would be hard to know where to find one, unless there was a retired priest or other associated minister attending church or otherwise known there. I know this because my colleagues call me for this type of work, because I advertise as a Free Range Priest.

I know that in order for this ministry to benefit more congregations, big and small, there needs to be an idea that this kind of work is available. There needs to be a way for congregations to contact clergy when they are in need of it, and clergy to offer it. A ministry like United Faith Leaders serves this purpose. A change in concept around where and how clergy serve could include this kind of service, or something similar set up within a denomination.

Small congregations, big choices

St. Paul's, like many similar churches, is at a crossroads. It is possible that this community will not survive more than another few years, and this could happen no matter what kind of relationship they have with a clergyperson. Yet this place, which has sustained its ministry into three centuries, also has the foundation of the Gospel and a history of perseverance that might see it through for another hundred years or so. Only time will tell. They do have their story, which includes coming to moments like these at fairly regular intervals, and at each one, taking the turn that seems the most faithful and often the most innovative. That their first priest started a mill to support both the church and the families that filled its pews is a sign of a community endowed with a sense of practical innovation. And survival.

Working with a Free Range Priest may be part of that current endowment - a way to meld the spiritual needs of a small group with the practical situation it finds itself in today. This is not too far off from the idea of putting people to work so they could stay in the community in the late 19th century. In order for the church to continue to survive and thrive, locally and globally, it does seem like congregations everywhere will have to make similar choices about their future. They will have to reconsider their own ministry and mission, where it is leading them and where it is currently hampering them. Free Range Priest ministry can be part of those conversations, and could potentially support that revisioning into the future.

Another part of this discernment is the denominational structure around them. St. Paul's is not considering their future alone, they have assistance from the diocese and support from the structures set up to help small congregations. Other denominations have similar support, and similar challenges, for promoting and protecting the ministry of the small church.

Free Range Priest ministry is not the answer to everything. But it is one way to consider options for the future of traditional congregational ministry, especially in places where that model is not thriving as it once was. It is also a way that denominational authorities can reconsider what supporting ordained ministry looks like. This may require some re-thinking of traditional clergy service and how this new model might fit into the kinds of oversight a denomination offers to all who serve within it. This includes how clergy get paid, and what constitutes full and part-time ministry from the denominational perspective.

It may take a shift in mindset, but it could bring new opportunities for congregations and clergy. It could offer clergy opportunities to better support themselves serving in ministry both inside and outside of the traditional model. It could offer life-giving options for congregations like St. Paul's.

8. Bye-bye 'Bi-vocational'!

I have to confess, as a priest, I have a so-called "trigger word." A word that sets me into spasms of irrational rage, followed by ranting. My friends know not to use this word around me, unless they want to endure a litany of all that is wrong in the church and the world.

That word is *bi-vocational*.

I am just fine when it is used in its literal sense, to describe an ordained person who also works in another field. Someone who has more than one calling. I have known many bi-vocational clergy: those who serve as teachers, farmers, doctors, etc. as well as in the church. These are people who bring their gifts back and forth across disciplines, making connections between them. Those who serve this way do so because they feel equally called to more than one profession.

I know a priest who is also a surgeon. He takes both vocations quite seriously, serving a church on Sundays and a heavy rotation in a hospital during the week. He also works in medical ethics, bringing insights and experiences from one realm to another. I am impressed with how he fulfills two callings at the same time. This is not the kind of ministry that upsets me.

Where I lose my mind is when someone calls ministry *bi-vocational* when what they really mean is: "you will not be paid for your work." Another word for this, which also drives me to distraction, is *tentmaking*, taken from the Acts of the Apostles:

"After this Paul left Athens and went to Corinth. There he found a Jew named Aquila, a native of Pontus, who had recently come from Italy with his wife Priscilla, because Claudius had ordered all Jews to leave Rome. Paul went to see them, and, because he was of the same trade, he stayed with them, and they worked together—by trade they were tentmakers. Every sabbath he would argue in the synagogue and would try to convince Jews and Greeks." (Acts 18:1-4).

These few verses are from the Biblical book that documents what happens to the followers of Jesus after his ascension into heaven. How the news of resurrection and the coming of God's Kingdom spread across modern Italy, Greece, Northern Africa, and beyond in a relatively short amount of time. The reason this particular snippet of Scripture is often quoted is because it refers to the Apostle Paul working a secular job, ostensibly to supplement his extensive ministry getting the whole Christian church started.

Tentmaking is used today to describe someone who works in ministry and has another job in order to pay the bills. Because Paul did it, tentmaking is seen as something that has been part of the life of the church since its very beginning. It is often used as proof that ministers who are supported solely by the congregation are more the exception than the rule, historically speaking. It establishes that from the very beginning of Christianity itself, *if* ministers get paid, *what* they get paid, and by *whom*, have been questions we all must contend with.

Which is why I get so worked up over this, and *bi-vocational*, when it is used in the sense of clergy not receiving compensation. It is glossing over important considerations, mostly that clergy generally *do* need to be paid in order to support themselves and their families. It also suggests that the work clergy do is not worth compensation, and therefore that what we do is not valued. It hides within it all the systematic issues about congregations and their ability to support clergy in their ministry. To me, it puts an end to an extremely important conversation we should be having as the church.

If we decide ordained ministry is free, then we avoid finding solutions that might allow clergy and congregations to address these issues together. We also create other problems, such as deciding why some ministry is paid for and some is not. It is a slippery slope all the way down to why we pay clergy at all. It leads ultimately to whether we will continue to have ordained ministers, if none can afford to sustain themselves. Both *bi-vocational* and *tentmaking* imply that this might be the case.

Regardless of how it is described, serving simultaneously in the secular and sacred realms is on the rise, for reasons noted all throughout this book. Since so many congregations cannot support full or even part-time ministry, clergy must get paid doing other work in order to continue to serve in them. As church attendance goes down, tentmaking ministry goes up. Even though there is a great deal of discussion about whether this is a good[56] thing or a bad[57] thing, everyone pretty much agrees it is, indeed, a thing. That more and more often today, there is just not enough money for an ordained minister in church, and few, if any, other opportunities be paid for clergy work.

I don't believe that the answer is not paying for ministry at all.

Free Range Priest ministry aims to make us all "uni-vocational" if we want to be. Ideally, everyone should be able to find satisfying work that compensates them fairly. Clergy are no exception. The concept of Free Range Priest is that clergy can have multiple jobs, but one ministry. This can happen outside the traditional congregational model, within it, or as a combination of both.

There are implications for the wider church if we continue to allow *bi-vocational* to be misused and misunderstood. For clergy, it can mean not being able to continue to serve the church. If congregations don't have to pay for ministry, they certainly won't seek to. At a time when there are fewer positions available overall, there will be even fewer for clergy who must be paid for their work in order to make ends meet.

For congregations, this can change how we value ministry. Already in the Episcopal Church, there is sometimes a sense of "two-tiered" ordination, an informal distinction made between those with and without seminary education. Sacramentally, there is no difference between us - ordination bestows the same gifts and responsibilities no matter how a candidate has been formed. But practically, we do sometimes act as if there is a difference, and it is manifested in salary. Non-stipendiary clergy are rarely those who went to seminary. Conversely, some dioceses set policy that denies compensation to priests who are not seminary graduates. Despite the fact that all our ordinations are equally valid, this literally places a different value on the work of some.

Finally, in the larger world, we risk not having clergy at all if we cannot afford to support what they do. In a day when we are in such need of *more* Christian evangelism, teaching, and community, we should be paying clergy more for their work. As it is, many find it daunting to consider years of formation, education and training that may well lead to ordination, but will still require another job for support. We can't be too surprised if some excellent candidates for ministry decline their call because they cannot afford to follow it.

Becoming a Free Range Priest is an alternative that makes ministry affordable *for* congregations and affordable *to* clergy. It is part of the conversation about clergy compensation that the church has been having since it began.

Back in the day

Despite how often people quote Paul in terms of being a tentmaker, the idea of clergy working both secular and sacred jobs has become more prevalent in modern times. Before that, there were several ways that clergy managed to make a living while also serving the church. A few generations ago, for instance, it was common for churches to have rectories (or vicarages, parsonages or manses) - houses on their property where the priest or minister and his family could live (and in those days, it was exclusively "his").

In this way, clergy got the extra benefit of free housing and congregations did not have to come up with more cash to compensate them. This system had definite pluses and minuses, but worked reasonably well as long as the congregation could afford the upkeep of the house, and as long as clergy wanted to live there. This system also worked for congregations because the clergyperson's wife was usually present, living on the grounds of the church, and providing a great deal of unpaid work for the community herself.

The Episcopal Church has roots in England, where this system was even more complex. Wealthy families usually left the bulk of their estate to their firstborn son, and sons born after that pretty much got nothing. This prompted more than a few of them to become clergy, where at least they got a "living" (basically, a house). Ensconced there, they were usually well-fed and tended to by members of their congregations[58].

This trend spread to America and across denominations in the 18th and 19th century, so that while clergy still did not get paid very much, they had a place to live. Since they served in a community, the community took it upon themselves to provide food and other kinds of extra-financial support for them. Clergy kids often saw the doctor for low fees or got into better schools than they normally would, and parishioners took it upon themselves to keep up the house where they lived. The issue of compensation was not straightforward in terms of compensation, benefits, etc., but the tangible and intangible "extras" helped clergy and their families live comfortably.

The remnants of this system can be seen most clearly today in the Roman Catholic Church, although pay and housing for its priests comes mainly from the denomination, rather than each congregation. Since Roman priests have historically been celibate (an exception allows some to be married today), it has been easier to provide rectories than extra pay for housing. There are also funds and facilities through the Roman Catholic Church to take care of its priests when they retire, and to help defray other living expenses[59].

In the 19th and 20th centuries, denominations in the US started establishing pension funds, as they realized that once clergy left their church housing and the general care of a congregation, their meager savings did not get them very far, and they were in real danger of poverty. So this benefit was added to help support clergy who generally did not own their own property and did not get paid a very high wage. This has been a huge help to clergy. At the same time, it can be harder on congregations, who must bear the additional expense of adding into the pension on behalf of their clergy.

This all appears to have worked well into the 1960s, the turning point for mainline Christian denominations to be able to support clergy through housing and pension added to a relatively small salary. As time went on, with rising property costs and falling congregational membership, it became harder to make this work. Many rectories were sold off because the church could no longer afford them. Clergy also wanted their own their own houses, which gave them equity and a little psychological and spiritual distance from the congregation.

The mid-20th century was also when women were ordained in several mainline denominations. With this, the expectations for both clergy and their spouses transformed. It became the norm that a minister's spouse, whether male or female, would have a career of their own, and perhaps not be so available for work in the church. And where a clergyperson lived was not solely determined by proximity to the church. Other factors, like a spouse's workplace, or children's school, became more important as well.

With these changes, people began to consider ordained ministry as a professional vocation, like law or medicine. If clergy didn't live on the grounds of the church, and if they and their families had multiple professional and personal obligations, that meant a whole new concept of the relationship between clergy and congregation. This meant new discussions of hours the clergyperson would work, days off and vacation time, professional development and standards. The concept of ministry began to take on a feel of work in a way it had not before. Salaries began to be rise, because fewer clergy were living in church housing, and because the vocation was seen in more professional ways.

All of this added new complexity to the issues of how clergy get paid and what happens when congregations cannot afford to pay them enough to live on. Today there are relatively few rectories, and they exist primarily in areas where the cost of housing is prohibitive (lots of them are in New York City). Often only the most historically wealthy denominations - like Episcopalians - could afford them. Pensions still exist for those who serve in mainline denominations, but they are becoming ever more burdensome for congregations. Now, in the 21st century, we have reached a point where professional-level salaries and compensation are things that half our congregations struggle to provide for clergy. And we are not equipped to go back to the days when clergy's needs were mostly provided by the congregation. So we are heading all the way back to where we were when Paul was making tents.

Bi-vocational and *tentmaking* are terms born out of addressing the economic reality of traditional church model. Congregations support the whole system - buildings and their upkeep, clergy salary and benefits, all other ministry - through member giving almost exclusively. Sometimes there are just not enough people in the community, or they don't have enough to give, to keep up with it all. Having clergy willing and able to serve for free seems like a gift. It is a complicated one, however. The more it happens, the less able we are to find more systematic solutions, and clergy have fewer choices in their ministry. Ultimately this means congregations have fewer choices, as well.

Some clergy have the gifts for working in two different worlds. They want to be tentmakers, and there are certainly positive aspects to their type of ministry. There is a whole mission field in the secular world and sometimes more job security, if they keep a foot there and a foot in ministry. But too often, clergy feel they have no choice but to work a non-church job if they want to remain in ministry and support themselves. Bi-vocational should be ministry that we feel truly called to, not a necessity.

Many congregations and denominations still manage to pay their clergy living wages, but the system is definitely changing. Even the tax-free housing allowance, a vestige of the time most clergy lived in church-owned housing, is now increasingly up for debate. It is no wonder clergy are increasingly grappling with the idea of tentmaking to pay their bills and live into their vocation. But some are finding that they can and do make their living exclusively in ministry, even if it is not all in the same place, or for the same congregation.

In this way, being a Free Range Priest is nothing new - many ordained ministers are already serving their vocation in several different ministries simultaneously. What is new is the idea of claiming this *as* our ministry. This is not something must do to make our way, not an exception as a way to make a living. Free Range Priest ministry can be exactly what we are called to in order to have just one ministry. Working in more than one place can add up to one true vocation.

Clergy can and should be paid for ministry

Like many professionals, and many clergy, I have a profile on LinkedIn, the business social media site. There I keep up with my own resume and browse others, mostly out of curiosity about what my friends are up to. LinkedIn often sends its users suggestions of jobs we might be interested in, or people who might be looking to hire those with certain skills, and I get them occasionally. Lately, the jobs that LinkedIn thinks I might be interested in are these: volunteer for the Muscular Dystrophy Association, volunteer for the Girl Scouts, volunteer for Catholic Charities... I have a master's degree and 20 years of experience working in the church, but this professional website thinks I am not qualified to be paid for my work!

I don't really blame them (or not too much, anyway). I think a lot of the things we do as clergy are not thought about as work - we listen, we comfort, we pray. We read and write and think. We sit with people and mourn with them and rejoice with them. We point to the presence of God. As we have discussed throughout this book, there is a strangeness to claiming and defining our work *as* work, since so much of it is spiritual in nature. It is hard to define, and it is harder, still, to talk about getting paid for. It is no wonder the business world does not highly value it! But it is important that *we* value it. And part of value, in our culture, is getting paid.

Even Paul had some things to say about this in the Bible, it turns out. When we talk about clergy doing secular work to supplement our ministry, we usually focus only on the verses from Acts that I shared above. Though it is true that Paul worked alongside the tentmakers he met in Corinth, he still thought that ministers deserved to be compensated, it turns out.

It is not even abundantly clear that the tentmaking Paul was doing in this one Bible story was out of necessity, because he needed to make ends meet, or simply out of his desire to create Christian community. He could very well have been working with the Corinthians because it was a way to get to know them, and to have them know and trust him, and the message he was bringing them about the Gospel. We don't know how long he was making tents there - it could have been just that one time. We do know that not long after this time, Paul sets sail for Syria, and points beyond, and never returns. Beyond this one line of Scripture, there is no consistent Biblical record of Paul working outside of his ministry.

There is, however, a Biblical record of Paul arguing that those in ministry should be paid for their work. In fact, coincidentally (or not), it also has to do with the church in Corinth. Later in his ministry, Paul wrote a series of letters to established churches, some of which are preserved as New Testament Scripture. In his First Letter to the Corinthians, he is plenty vexed with all manner of conflict among the members of this particular congregation (which, ironically, is where we find one of the most famous passages in the Bible, 1 Corinthians 13 - 'love is patient, love is kind', that we all know from weddings). Among the things he is angry about is the fact that some members of the congregation are complaining about having to pay the minister!

Paul is not at all pleased by this. In his own words... "Do I say this on human authority? Does not the law also say the same? For it is written in the law of Moses, 'You shall not muzzle an ox while it is treading out the grain.' Is it for oxen that God is concerned? Or does he not speak entirely for our sake? It was indeed written for our sake, for whoever plows should plow in hope and whoever threshes should thresh in hope of a share in the crop. If we have sown spiritual good among you, is it too much if we reap your material benefits? If others share this rightful claim on you, do not we still more?

"Nevertheless, we have not made use of this right, but we endure anything rather than put an obstacle in the way of the gospel of Christ. Do you not know that those who are employed in the temple service get their food from the temple, and those who serve at the altar share in what is sacrificed on the altar? In the same way, the Lord commanded that those who proclaim the gospel should get their living by the gospel." (1 Corinthians 9:8-14).

Yikes. Paul clearly has some feelings about minsters getting paid! He seems incensed at those who would suggest that sharing the Gospel is not an occupation entitled to compensation. It makes me feel better that *bi-vocational* was a trigger word for him, too.

The idea that Paul was a tentmaker, engaged in ministry and secular work at the same time - at least happily - complicated by these words. Scripture is open to interpretation, of course. It is certainly possible that Paul, and others, were paid part-time for ministry and part-time for secular work, whatever those terms meant in the first century Christian world. It also clearly establishes that the tension around who pays clergy, for what, and how much, has been around as long as Christianity has.

So the picture would be incomplete if we simply think that since Biblical times, ordained ministers have contentedly worked for little or no pay, and supplemented their income on the side. This may be true, or it may be partially true, but it seems more accurate to say we have been wrestling with this issue since Christianity itself began. I have no hopes of solving it once and for all today! I will say, though, that our work as ordained ministers is valuable, and it has always carried value in the world along with its spiritual benefits.

Tentmaking itself is ministry. Some clergy who do not technically have to work secular jobs out of necessity still do so for the experience. I have a colleague who works in a running store as well as pastoring a church. He told he he would not have it any other way, because he gets to talk to more people about Jesus. In fact, he says that he might have more conversations directly about faith when he is talking with runners than when he is at church. This boundary-crossing is a call of its own, and I am in complete support of it. What I do hope is that no clergy feel forced into additional secular work, or even out of ministry altogether, because they cannot make a living at it.

All of this still supports the idea that the work we should be compensated for what it is. The question has been with us since Biblical times. Even the ancient Jewish priests got to keep the meat that was sacrificed at the altar (Leviticus 6:26). Part of being a Free Range Priest is recognizing the value of our work and envisioning new, productive ways to live into it. It also means that we should not offer our ministry for free.

Many parts, one vocation

Many clergy do not have any issue with being paid for their work, they worry about *how* they will get paid. And churches don't pay for clergy because they can't afford salaries. We use words like *bi-vocational* and *non-stipendiary* when we mean un-compensated because sometimes it seems like the only choice.

But there are other ways to think about this, and other solutions for supporting ministry.

We have already seen some clergy who serve their callings outside the traditional model altogether. It is still ministry - still the work that clergy do - but they get paid for it online, by individuals and groups who are not technically members of a congregation or other institution. Some clergy do similar work, but within the institution, finding ways to serve in multiple places and get fully compensated. It is another way to understand Free Range Priest ministry.

The Rev. Cheryl Barton Henry is probably more like a Free Range *Pastor*, since she is a Presbyterian minister and this is a more fitting title. She is one of those adventurous clergy who has been answering God's call in lots of ways, over a long and impressive career. She is frank and down-to-earth, the very essence of someone you would turn to in a crisis, or your favorite person to share of cup of coffee with. I know this because we have been friends for over 25 years. So I usually just call her Cherrie.

Henry has, in some ways, had a traditional clergy trajectory, a career that has grown over time and place. She was ordained 30 years ago into a 700-member church in LaGrange, Georgia. She co-pastored a small, rural congregation in Calypso, North Carolina. She then spent 15 years as the campus minister at Duke University in Durham, North Carolina. Here she developed deep, life-long relationships with young adults from all over the world, and took them on mission trips to places such as Haiti and the Dominican Republic. Then she was ready for something new. "When the kids started getting to the age my own kids were, it was time for me to go," says this mother of two. "I started to worry more about protecting them than challenging them."

Henry has deep roots in Durham, however, including her husband's job and kids in school. So moving away for a new position did not seem optimal. The area around her, though, which includes several cities, a few universities, and a couple of highly respected divinity schools, makes it a challenging place for any ordained minister to find work. There are plenty of clergy living in this part of North Carolina, and the competition for ministry positions is quite high.

Henry was also not sure she wanted to take just any position that might be available - she has been ordained long enough to know her gifts and skills, and to want to serve where she feels called. So from there, she has made her own way, quite eclectically and successfully, listening to where God is leading her and pushing to make it work. She keeps her ties at Duke by leading spiritual formation groups for first year Divinity School students. She guest lectures and leads retreats, and also helps train field education supervisors. She still has friendship with former campus ministry students, now off in all parts of the country. Henry celebrates an impressive number of weddings in many different locations, along with offering pre-marital counseling for couples. She is available for pastoral counseling, especially to former students. She is a spiritual director.

Within the congregation, Henry serves 20 hours a week for a small Presbyterian church in Efland, North Carolina. She serves 10 hours a week at First Presbyterian Church in downtown Durham, where she works with young adults, offering pastoral care, some worship responsibilities, and some program work. She takes students to Montreat, a Presbyterian retreat center in the mountains of North Carolina, for a week every summer. She moderates a session (a small group of elders who make church decisions) at another rural church, not her own, and she supervises their pastor because he is still a student. Because of this, she also celebrates Communion for them once a month, since he is not yet ordained. Each year she supervises two field education students from Duke Divinity School.

This is the life of a Free Range Priest. Most of the places she serves could not afford to offer her a full-time salary. More importantly, she doesn't really want to serve in any of them exclusively. She enjoys being able to do a variety of work where she is able to offer her best gifts to serve God and others. Her ministry is serving in many different capacities.

It seems like Henry does everything, except get decently compensated. For all of this work, she makes about $37,000 a year - along with a contribution to the Presbyterian Pension Fund, which makes her total roughly $45,000. This seems like a very small salary for the amount of work she does. Indeed, it is less than the median US household income of $55,775[60]. This financial reality, to Henry, is the only drawback to the Free Range Priest work she has been doing these past several years.

She has, occasionally, considered full-time congregational or chaplaincy work as positions have come available. I asked her if she thought she would ever go back to full-time salaried work, and she said no.

"I love doing the ministry I have now, and I would keep doing it for sure, especially if I were making decent money. But I struggle theologically with the idea of justice in terms of what I get paid. I am clearly not getting paid what I deserve. I know I have a nice quality of life, and I lack for nothing. And I know that other people really struggle to make ends meet, and some live in poverty. Still, I don't think I am paid fairly for what I do."

One of the unintended consequences of not paying for some ordained ministry is the overall de-valuing of the work. If some do it for free, and some work many hours for very little, then it gets harder to consider what a fair wage is for someone like Henry, working on contract in several different places. If congregations cannot afford clergy salaries, there should be a way to help them pay a reasonable, sustainable rate for clergy time and task. This is true for other institutions and individuals within the church as well.

Henry works full-time, but gets paid less than the average Presbyterian minister[61], and less than the average elementary school teacher[62] (at nine months a year). Part of the challenge for all clergy, and definitely for those who work on contract, is to continue to get paid what our work is worth. Henry herself would love to make $30 an hour, for instance, which would put her salary in the $60,000 a year range. This is still below average for clergy in general, but around the median for US households. It is still a stretch for a lot of congregations, especially since $60,000 salary translates to around $100,000 when healthcare and pension benefits are added.

I think it is possible, though, to reach this via Free Range Priest ministry.

As Henry knows, because she is at the forefront of it, this kind of ministry is still emerging. Moving past *bi-vocational* and into contract work is a start, but it is still a challenge to make ends meet this way. I asked Henry for advice for any other aspiring Free Range Priests, she laughed and said, "Choose a good patron!" By this she means that she feels most fortunate that her husband, Andy, has a good stable job that takes some of the financial pressure off of her ("St. Andrew, my patron!"). In fact, all of the Free Range Priests I have spoken with, including Jabriel Ballentine, Lisa Cressman and Jay McNeal, mentioned their gratitude for spouses who support them in every way, including financially. The same is true for me.

Being a Free Range Priest means finding a place between *tentmaking* and full-time salaried compensation. It means that *bi-vocational* can go back to its literal meaning only, those who are called into more than one vocation. Clergy cannot do this alone, however. We rely on the changing attitudes and understanding of those who serve in the institutional church, those in the pews, and those in denominational oversight.

The wider conversation

As part of my own ministry, I served on a bishop's staff. My job was to support congregations and clergy across the geographical boundaries within a larger diocese. Those boundaries for me included one of the fastest growing areas in the country, the Raleigh/Durham/Chapel Hill 'Triangle' of North Carolina, and some of the smallest towns and poorest counties in the state. Throughout all of this territory there are many Episcopal churches.

Because of the history of how North Carolina was settled, and how it grew, the eastern part is dotted with tiny congregations a day's horseback ride apart. The further west in the state you go - until the mountains - the more distance between churches, because the population grew later and transportation became easier. Today the vast majority of people live in the center, between Charlotte and Raleigh, but many small churches remain in the wide open, sparsely populated distance between the Triangle and the beach.

Part of my job was to help figure out the best way for some of those tiny congregations to be served by clergy. Another part was to help clergy, most of whom live near the urban centers of the state, find places to serve. The time I spent doing this was invaluable in terms of getting a bird's-eye view of the needs across the church, and some sense of what might have to change in order for ministry to continue to thrive, and to grow in new ways.

Serving in my diocesan capacity meant countless hours driving back and forth across the state. One thing I always noticed, besides the coyotes and eagles, was how many churches I passed. Many towns I visited had fewer than 500 inhabitants, but even these had at least one Baptist church, one Methodist, one Roman Catholic, one non-denominational, and one Spanish-speaking congregation. Many had two of each, because of deep historical class and race divides. Everyone in town could attend one of these congregations and still they would all be small. And most of them would still be served by clergy who lived at least 50 miles away.

It made me wonder what kind of conversations, if any, about supporting ministry happened between these churches.

I also spent time serving in the Episcopal Diocese of Kansas, which covers vast swaths of beautiful, essentially uninhabited space. Congregations there tend not just to be small, but also isolated. The population of the whole state of Kansas is only three times larger than the city I live in. Not surprisingly, there are also fewer clergy in Kansas than in other areas of the country. Supporting clergy and congregational ministry is even harder when the challenges are greater. I am a little more familiar with the conversations happening here between different denominations about how to support clergy and make sure that congregations have access to ordained ministry.

I have some understanding of why *bi-vocational* ministry persists as a description of unpaid clergy service. In some places, it really is a choice between not paying for ordained ministry and not having it at all. Yet this is what also led me to Free Range Priest ministry. It seems impossible to believe that this is a long-term solution to the challenges facing the church.

I wonder how the conversation across the church might change if we simply insisted that clergy must be paid for their work. It might mean that some churches would have to close, or that some clergy would not have places to serve. It might also open other possibilities we have not thought of yet. Some of them exist already, and some of them can and will bring new life to the church.

In my work on the diocesan level, I got to see how immediate issues - keeping churches open, finding jobs for clergy, keeping the Gospel shared in as many ways as possible - could take up all our time and energy. We did not always have a lot left over to gain perspective on the bigger picture or the longer term. I started to see how Free Range could mean the space to take a step back and consider how many different pieces there are to this very large puzzle of all that is changing in the church today.

My own vision is the piece I have to share. I know that many conversations are going on right now in denominational leadership: about the future of the church, about supporting clergy, about how to do ministry in new ways. I know they are going on between denominations, as well. And I know there are lots of ways these conversations will continue. Within them, I think there is room to talk about Free Range Priest ministry.

In 2016 I led a workshop at the Cooperative Baptist Convention in Winston-Salem, NC. I spoke with several clergy there about their own ministry and some of their concerns about being able to support themselves. Their denominational structure is not as extensive as the one in the Episcopal Church, and they could not count on some of the things I take for granted as a priest, such as minimum salary requirements and a pension. They were extremely excited to talk about what it means to be a Free Range Priest. It seems to me that even extending the conversation is a way to support ministry.

The Free Range Priest vocation

The Apostle Paul was the first Free Range Priest. Paul traveled the world, moving from country to country and congregation to congregation with only one goal - sharing the Good News of Jesus Christ and supporting the church in its ministry. He was obviously compensated in some way - whether or not he got a salary, he was interested in collecting money from people for support of the early church and the minsters who served it. He accepted lodging and food from various disciples and communities. He even made some tents.

But all his work was directly in service to his one and only vocation - evangelist, teacher, counselor, exhorter and celebrator of the Christian faith. Today we call it ordained ministry. Paul may have gotten paid from a variety of sources, in a variety of ways, and for a variety of jobs, but he really only did one thing. He was called a tentmaker in one chapter of his life story. He lives in our tradition as our foundational Apostle.

This is why I struggle with the term *bi-vocational*. I am passionately committed to the idea that clergy can and should be compensated for our work. I am equally committed to the idea that congregations should not be overburdened trying to do this. And my passion extends to helping clergy find ways to serve in the wider community. I think we can follow in Paul's footsteps and make one ministry out of a variety of work. I am already doing it myself.

As I speak more about being a Free Range Priest, some people have suggested that it is hardly a change at all from the way we have always done things. Others think it is truly radical. I think it is a little bit of both, and the best part of it so far is how people are really interested in talking about it. There is energy around the idea of simply thinking about what ordained ministry can and does look like in the world, and the church, today.

Just the simple questions: "what about this is ministry?", "what do we pay a priest for?", "how could we do this better?", "where is God calling us?" offer many new ideas for the traditional church model, and beyond. Some of these might require risk, courage, and change.

Many professions and institutions are undergoing changes in the beginning of this new century. In other systems, those devoted to the mission are asking themselves how to keep the valuable core of what they do and also think about it apart from the way it currently gets done. What is the product and what is the process? How can technology make things easier? What is keeping us from our goal and what could we change to get there?

Church, in this sense, is not that much different. We have something valuable to share - the transforming love of Jesus Christ - and we must ask the questions about how we share it. The traditional model doesn't work like it used to. How can we support it where it works, and transform where it needs to?

My hope is that Free Range Priest ministry is one small way of being part of this transformation.

Conclusion

My favorite book of the Bible is the Acts of the Apostles. It is the story about what happens after Jesus is risen from the dead, appears to his followers, instructs them to go baptize and make disciples in his name, then ascends into heaven. His bewildered friends are left literally staring up into the sky, wondering what is happening and what they will do without him.

With the help of the Holy Spirit, they do ok. The Book of Acts starts out strong, with the formation of the Christian church, thousands converted to this new faith, and disciples healing and raising people from the dead. They keep their belongings in common, share Scripture, stories and meals, repent of their sins and baptize each other as followers of Jesus. They work out the beliefs and practices of this new religion. Paul, the persecutor of Christians, is converted and becomes chief evangelist, and he and Peter clash over whether members must be Jews before they become Christian (it turns out they don't). It is exciting stuff, and seems to be one success after another.

This all happens in the first half of Acts, though. Eventually, the story moves into a fairly predictable pattern of following Paul on his adventures to convert those in other lands. He is repeatedly arrested, beaten, and jailed. He suffers illness, hunger, shipwreck and snake bite. The conversions are smaller and less dramatic, the dangers and setbacks are ever more real. Even in the first generation of Christianity, things don't go all that smoothly for very long. Finally, the book doesn't so much end as it just kind of trails off in Chapter 28, with Paul once again arrested and defending the faith, this time in Rome.

For a long time, I was perplexed as to why there is no neat conclusion to the Acts of the Apostles, no big wrap-up or take-home message for the church. Then, when I was in seminary, my New Testament professor said this is because we are all the 29th chapter. Until Jesus comes again, we are still writing the book.

It's not like Christianity is over and now we are watching endless loops of the highlights. It is century after century of living our stories and sharing the faith. All the glory and the heartache that comes with it. I have always loved this.

The Christian Church feels like the most solid thing in the world to those of us who were raised in it, who serve God and each other through it. But it is also changing all the time - living and breathing with us, handed down by us, subject to persecution at times, but growing just the same. We are still part of the chapter of what it looks like for groups of people to follow Jesus, and it is still full of adventure. So every time it looks perplexing, we are just turning another page.

My own faith adventure has always been about a call to the priesthood. I didn't always know that, but I am more sure of it as I get older and see the many ways my life was set up on this path. I was raised in the Roman Catholic Church and educated by Jesuits. In fact, I like to say that the Jesuits turned me into an Episcopalian, because they encouraged me to listen for God's voice. When I heard it, and it was about ordination, my mentors never doubted it, even though the Roman Catholic Church does not ordain women. When I was ordained by the Episcopalians, I received a beautiful letter of congratulations and support from my former English professor, himself a Jesuit priest.

Ordained ministry has also been part of my story for generations. My grandfather's sister, Emily Caimano (aka Sr. Rose Acquin), was a Dominican nun in Blauvent, NY. She earned a PhD and was the author of a book on mystic spirituality[63]. She was writing it when I was born. My grandfather, Nicholas Caimano, Sr., was an attorney in Albany, NY. Just before he died, while I was in seminary in the late 1990's, he told me that he had been called to the priesthood as well. But soon afterwards he met my grandmother, and his love for her prevented him from answering it. Still, I walked in his footsteps.

On my mother's side, my grandmother's family was Methodist. I recently learned that my great-grandmother's sister, Belle Evans Haas, was a minister in rural Missouri, in an era when it was not so common for women to be ordained. Coincidentally, I also married a Haas, although I am assured we are not actually related.

All this convinces me that I am a priest to my very bones. It gives me confidence in following God's call to bear the sacraments and traditions of the Christian faith. It helps me see that my own story is a small but not insignificant part of the larger 29th chapter of the Acts of the Apostles.

I feel fortunate that my priesthood has straddled centuries. I was formed and educated for ordination in an era when the traditional model of church was still assumed. When I was in seminary, there was no talk, or any concept, that being a priest meant anything besides serving as a full-time congregational pastor. A few of us might have been also called to be professors or musicians, some might eventually become bishops, but *priest* meant serving in a church, tending to a flock. All my thoughts about what the future would look like included an altar, a pulpit, a stone church, and one group of people gathered there on Sunday.

Of course, it might still look like that, if I hadn't decided that God was calling me in another direction. If I had not been opened to all the changes happening in this new century. Some things still work like they used to, and some churches are just as sturdy as they have been for the past 100 years. But enough has changed that I can clearly see what we are losing, and what we still have to gain. The chapter we are writing as the church today goes on, despite how we might want to stay only with the moments when the Spirit is strong, the direction is clear. The next adventure is before us.

Because I am a priest, I see the path in terms of priesthood. I want to be part of the conversation about how valuable our work is, in so many ways. I think this conversation can also be good for everyone in the church, and everyone who hasn't heard the Gospel yet. I am so grateful for the many others who see things in different terms, whose work is helping them spread good news in whatever way they are called.

And I am excited to be in this place where I have enough experience being a priest of the 20th century, and enough vision to be a priest of the 21st century. At least that is my hope. So far, enough has aligned on my path that I feel I can trust in the next step.

In my mind, I see Free Range Priests serving all across the church, among and between denominations. I see us helping small congregations to survive and thrive, wherever they are. I see us lending our gifts to larger congregations in supportive ways. I see us finding new ways to bring the Gospel to all those who have never heard it before. I see us getting paid for our work, and supporting ourselves and our families doing what we love. I see the church moving forward in so many ways we can't see yet, as it has for all of the centuries before us. I expect to be surprised.

In the meantime, if you need me, you can find me in the pulpit or at the altar of some church, somewhere. Or you can find me online. Or whatever the next page in the chapter looks like. Still looking for new ways to follow Jesus.

[1] This is a real church in a real town, but I have changed the name.

[2] Episcopal Domestic Fast Facts: 2014. episcopalchurch.org.

[3] The 2014 Church Compensation Report. cpg.org.

[4] C. Kirk Hadaway. **Episcopal Congregations Overview: Findings from 2014 Survey of Episcopal Congregations**. episcopalchurch.org/research.

[5] Baptist Press. 'SBC reports more churches, fewer people.' bpnews.net.

[6] Sam Hodges. 'Part-time pastors claiming more pulpits'. The People of the United Methodist Church. umc.org.

[7] Gallup online research. In depth: Topics A To Z, Religion. gallup.com.

[8] Christian Smith. 'On 'Moralistic Therapeutic Deism'. Princeton Theological Seminary. ptsem.edu.

[9] Christian Smith. 'On 'Moralistic Therapeutic Deism'. Princeton Theological Seminary. ptsem.edu.

[10] Jonathan Vespa, Jamie M. Lewis and Rose M. Kreider. 'America's Families and Living Arrangements:2012.' August 2013. census.gov.

[11] D'Vera Conn, Jeffrey S. Passel, Wendy Wang and Gretchen Livingston. 'Barely Half of U.S. Adults are Married - A Record Low.' Pew Research Center, December 14, 2011. pewsocialtrends.org.

[12] 'Desmond Tutu'. Wikipedia.org.

[13] 'Martin Luther King, Jr.' Wikipedia.org.

[14] 'Presiding Bishop Michael Curry.' episcopalchurch.org.

[15] C. Kirk Hadaway and P.L. Marler. 'Did you really go to church this week? Behind the poll data'. The Christian Century, May 6, 1998. religion-online.org.

[16] "How Churches Serve Their Communities." Managing Your Church blog (churchlawandtax.com), December 11, 2012.

[17] Mike Clawson, "What Churches Contribute to the Community," Friendly Atheist blog (Patheos.com), March 21, 2011.

[18] Thom S. Rainer. 'How Many Hours Must a Pastor Work to Satisfy the Congregation?' July. 24, 2013. thomrainer.com.

[19] Rae Jean Proeschold-Bell, PhD. 'An Overview of the History and Current Status of Clergy Health'. Duke Global Health Institute Duke University Center for Health Policy and Inequalities Research. 2012.

[20] Into Action: From Seminary to Ministry. into-action.net.

[21] C. Kirk Hadaway. **Episcopal Congregations Overview: Findings from 2014 Survey of Episcopal Congregations**. episcopalchurch.org/research.

[22] C. Kirk Hadaway. **Episcopal Congregations Overview: Findings from 2014 Survey of Episcopal Congregations**. episcopalchurch.org/research.

[23] Scott Gunn. 'Episco-upgrades: Change clergy transitions'. April 27, 2010. sevenwholedays.org.

[24] C. Kirk Hadaway. **Episcopal Congregations Overview: Findings from 2014 Survey of Episcopal Congregations**. episcopalchurch.org/research.

[25] Matthew J. Price and Anne Hurst. 'The 2014 Church Compensation Report: A National, Provincial and Diocesan Analysis of Clergy Compensation.' June 2015. episcopalchurch.org.

[26] C. Kirk Hadaway. **Episcopal Congregations Overview: Findings from 2014 Survey of Episcopal Congregations**. episcopalchurch.org/research.

[27] C. Kirk Hadaway. **Episcopal Congregations Overview: Findings from 2014 Survey of Episcopal Congregations**. episcopalchurch.org/research.

[28] Anthony Ruger, Sharon L. Miller and Kim Maphis Early. "The Gathering Storm: The Educational Debt of Theological Students". Auburn Studies, No. 12, September 2005.

[29] "U.S. Cities are Home to 62.7 Percent of the U.S. Population, but Comprise Just 3.5 Percent of the Land Area." United States Census Bureau, March 04, 2015. Census.gov.

[30] C. Kirk Hadaway. **Episcopal Congregations Overview: Findings from 2014 Survey of Episcopal Congregations**. episcopalchurch.org/research.

[31] Brian Kaylor. "Rural churches struggle as resources flow to urban churches." Baptist Global News. November 12, 2015. Baptistnews.com.

[32] Episcopal Domestic Fast Facts: 2014. episcopalchurch.org.

[33] Thad Austin. "Giving USA 2016: What Church Leaders Need to Know." June 24, 2016. seedbed.com.

[34] Biz Carson. 'How 3 guys turned renting an air mattress in their apartment into a $25 billion company.' Business Insider, Feb. 23, 2016.

[35] 'When Strangers Meet: An Airbnb Love Story'. blog.airbnb.com.

[36] Gallup online research. In depth: Topics A To Z, Religion. gallup.com.

[37] Elissa Gootman, 'The Officiant Among Us,' the New York Times. March 9, 2012.

[38] Davis, Simon. 'How Secular Americans are reshaping funeral rituals.' RNS, Religious News Service, December 17, 2015.

[39] American Association for Marriage and Family Therapy. aamft.org.

[40] Elizabeth Weil. 'The Unexpected Bat Mitzvah'. The New York Times. October 10, 2015.

[41] 'Personal Trainers in the US: Market Research Report.' IBIS World. October 2015.

[42] Dan Edmonds. "More than Half of College Faculty are Adjuncts: Should you Care?" Forbes Magazine. May 28, 2015. Forbes.com.

[43] Randall Frederick. "The State of Seminary Education." Theology & the City. November 19, 2015. theologyandthecity.com.

[44] Jordan Friedman. "Study: Enrollment in Online Education Up, Except at For-Profits." U.S. News and World Report. February 9, 2016. usnews.com.

[45] Tom Tanner and Eliza Smith Brown. "Why 100 ATS member schools have grown." The Association of Theological Schools. March 31, 2015. ats.edu.

[46] "Chris Yaw: Every congregation can have an online school." Faith and Leadership. May 19, 2015. faithandleadership.com.

[47] firstnationministry.org.

[48] Brendon Schrader. 'Here's Why the Freelancer Economy is on the Rise' FastCompany.com. August 10, 2015.

[49] Allen Webster Joslin, BA, STM, MA, Vicar. 'Saint Paul's Chestnut Hill Salisbury, North Carolina: An Historical Sketch.' June 7, 1987 (self-published), p.3.

[50] Allen Webster Joslin, BA, STM, MA, Vicar. 'Saint Paul's Chestnut Hill Salisbury, North Carolina: An Historical Sketch.' June 7, 1987 (self-published), p.6.

[51] Allen Webster Joslin, BA, STM, MA, Vicar. 'Saint Paul's Chestnut Hill Salisbury, North Carolina: An Historical Sketch.' June 7, 1987 (self-published), p.16.

[52] Allen Webster Joslin, BA, STM, MA, Vicar. 'Saint Paul's Chestnut Hill Salisbury, North Carolina: An Historical Sketch.' June 7, 1987 (self-published), p.7.

[53] Matthew J. Price and Anne Hurst. *The 2014 Church Compensation Report: A National, Provincial, and Diocesan Analysis of Clergy Compensation.* The Church Pension Group. June 2015.

[54] C. Kirk Hadaway. **Episcopal Congregations Overview: Findings from 2014 Survey of Episcopal Congregations**. episcopalchurch.org/research.

[55] Episcopal Domestic Fast Facts: 2014. episcopalchurch.org.

[56] Thom S. Rainer. 'Eight Characteristics of the New Bivocational Pastor.' January 18, 2026. thomrainer.com.

[57] Beau Underwood. 'The Dangers of Bi-Vocational Ministry.' July 30, 2014. Sojourners.org.

[58] Maria Grace. 'Vicars and curates and livings... oh my!' englishhistoryauthors.blogspot.com.

[59] 'What is the average salary of a Catholic priest in an average American parish?' Quora.com.

[60] Department of Numbers: US Household Income. deptofnumbers.com.

[61] Clergy Effective Salaries Compared by Congregation Size and Years of Service. pensions.org.

[62] Elementary School Salary Information US News .pdf money.usnews.com.

[63] Emily Mary Caimano. Mysticism in Gabriela Mistral: a clarification. PhD Thesis Dissertation, St. John's University, 1967.

I am entirely grateful for the love and support of all who encourage me, and especially the writing of this book. Thank you to all those who let me write about them in these pages, their amazing lives and ministries. To friends and strangers who have listened to me talk endlessly about being a Free Range Priest, even when they had no idea what that meant. To the amazing and fabulous *Beth Grace* for your editing gifts.

Not all my friends are required to be clergy, but it turns out most of them are.

To the Reverends:
Sarah Ball-Damberg, for all the runs, wine, and popcorn
Michael Buerkel Hunn, for giving me most of my good ideas
Lauren Winner, for helping me believe I am a writer
Betty Glover, for endless phone calls and humor
Cherrie Henry, for 25 years of walks around East Campus
Jessee Neal and *Peter Faass*, for the third week of July for the past 20 years.

To my family, especially my mom, *Barbara Caimano*, who always told me I would write a book someday. And to my godson *RJ Vogt*, aunt *Jo Vogt* and cousin *Lauren Caimano Nelson*, who remind me that we all need a priest in the family.

To pretty much every congregation and the entire staff of the Episcopal Diocese of North Carolina, who taught me everything I know - and put up with me thinking I know more than I do. Special thanks for the churches I served, who loved and formed me into a priest who at least knows something: the Church of the Holy Trinity, New York, NY; St. Philip's Episcopal Church, Durham, NC; and St. John's Episcopal Church, Wichita, KS.

To the Fleet Feet Huntersville running group, who help me talk about something besides church sometimes.

To *Kevin*, *Maggie*, and *Tyler* who make my house a home. And to *Jeff* for everything.

CPSIA information can be obtained
at www.ICGtesting.com
Printed in the USA
BVOW04s1912070517
483442BV00001B/43/P

9 781365 869235